# UNIFORMS & INSIGNIA OF
# THE NAVIES OF WORLD WAR II

# UNIFORMS & INSIGNIA OF THE NAVIES OF WORLD WAR II

Compiled by US Naval Intelligence

Introduction by Andrew Mollo

Greenhill Books, London

This edition of
*Uniforms & Insignia of the Navies of World War II*
first published 1991 by Greenhill Books, Lionel Leventhal Limited,
Park House, 1 Russell Gardens, London NW11 9NN

This edition and Introduction © Lionel Leventhal Limited, 1991
Plates 78–96 © National Geographic

*British Library Cataloguing in Publication Data*
Uniforms and insignia of the navies of World War II: Compiled
by US Naval Intelligence.
1. Navy. Uniforms, history   2. Navies. Insignia, history
359.1409

ISBN 1-85367-097-9

Printed by Colorcraft Ltd., Hong Kong

# CONTENTS

Introduction by Andrew Mollo                                    9

────────────────────── *The Plates:* ──────────────────────

| | | | |
|---|---|---|---|
| Argentine Navy | 17 | Royal Netherlands Navy | 73 |
| Brazilian Navy | 23 | Portuguese Navy | 79 |
| British Navy | 29 | Russian Navy | 82 |
| French Navy | 41 | Spanish Navy | 87 |
| German Navy | 47 | Swedish Navy | 90 |
| Greek Navy | 57 | Turkish Navy | 92 |
| Italian Navy | 60 | United States Navy, Marine | |
| Japanese Navy | 66 | Corps and Coast Guard | 94 |

# PUBLISHER'S NOTE

*Uniforms and Insignia of the Navies of World War II* is based upon *JAN1, Joint Army and Navy Publications, Uniforms and Insignia* (Washington, DC, 1943–5). All the plates in this volume are from *JAN1*, and the plates relating to the United States originated with and were included in *JAN1* by permission of the National Geographic. For this facsimile reproduction of the plates a new Introduction has been written by Andrew Mollo. *Uniforms and Insignia of the Navies of World War II* reproduces the plates in facsimile to the originals, and in five cases this shows lettering that has holes punched through, due to the loose-leaf nature of *JAN1*. The publishers wish to acknowledge the help of the National Geographic and Mr A. D. Baker III in making *Uniforms and Insignia of the Navies of World War II* possible.

# INTRODUCTION

*Uniforms and Insignia of the Navies of World War II* is based upon *Joint Army and Navy Publication Number One (JAN1)* and is the most comprehensive intelligence manual on military uniform to have been produced during World War II. As such it is much sought after by uniform specialists and bibliophiles and although rare and little known collectors will pay a high sum for it. This selected reissue of all the naval material contains 96 plates from *JAN1*, including 19 pages from the *National Geographic Magazine* special issues on Insignia and Decorations of the US Armed Forces, which first appeared in June 1943. These formed an integral part of the first issue of *JAN1* plates and were published by courtesy of the National Geographic Society.

Probably due, in part, to her pre-war isolationism the United States published more books on the identification of foreign uniforms and rank badges than any other country. Examples of such books are Blaksee's *Uniforms of the World*, which appeared in 1929, and Captain Bunkley's *Military and Naval Recognition Book*. In the 1930s the Germans also produced a series of coloured plates by the famous military artist Knötel and others, entitled *Soldiers of Europe (Die Soldaten Europas)*, designed to be displayed on walls of military establishments to promote awareness of the uniforms of the armed forces that ringed Germany. But neither in scope nor in detail did any of these works compare with the comprehensiveness of *JAN1*. The original work was produced in Washington, D.C. and one noticeable omission was the United States Navy. This was made good by the incorporation of the National Geographic plates. It is assumed that the original compilers did not consider it necessary to include details of US uniforms as American service personnel would already be familiar with them.

According to the original introduction, *JAN1* was published as a cumulative recognition manual of the uniforms used by the world's principal military powers. That portion dealing with army and air force uniforms was prepared by the Military Intelligence Service, while that illustrating naval uniforms was produced by the Naval Intelligence Division. It was intended as a rapid means of recognition for field use rather than an exhaustive manual on all possible uniforms. The document was unclassified and intended for official use only by the fighting forces and officials of the United Nations.

The loose-leaf format was chosen to permit the addition of new or revised material and allowed the user to add additional information published in the same format. Sheets included in this reprint are all individually dated, the earliest being February 1943 and the latest June 1945. A definitive list of all plates published has not yet come to light.

Coverage of Axis nations is confined to German, Italian and Japanese Navies, while plates on their allies (Bulgaria, Croatia, Finland, Hungary, Roumania and Manchuria) were probably in preparation but not, so far as is known, published. The British, French, Dutch, Greek and Soviet navies have been published, although by the time the manual appeared, the navies of many of the smaller nations had been reduced to national contingents serving with the British Royal Navy. Separate plates were not devoted to Britain's colonies and Dominions, whose personnel wore Royal Navy uniforms with minor national distinctions. The Soviet Navy, or Moscow Fleet as it was known in Russia, had recently re-introduced traditional rank badges in the form of shoulder-boards. The inclusion of plates of uniforms of the neutral countries (Argentina, Portugal, Spain, Sweden and Turkey) is useful because there is very little information in print on the uniforms of any of these countries – one wishes it might have been possible to include more.

It only takes a cursory glance at these plates to recognise those features of naval uniform that, through circumstance or tradition, had become almost universal and those that, while not universal, were common to groups of nations sharing a common heritage.

Head-dress can be divided into three basic types. Most sailors wore a hat with a soft crown and left the ends of their ribbon, or tally, long. Greek, Portuguese and Swedish sailors wore the British style, which was stiff, with the crown only marginally wider than the band; the cap tally was usually tied in a bow at the side. The third type was the US sailors' white fatigue cap, the popularity of which was such that it came to be worn on all occasions. This same cap was worn, as a fatigue hat, by Argentine, Brazilian and Portuguese sailors. During World War II a number of navies introduced various different types of working head-dress such as the beret or overseas cap or, as in both the German and Japanese navies, a naval version of a head-dress already in use in their respective armies.

Petty officers were distinguished from ratings by a peaked cap with a plain peak and a simple badge, and officers by a cap with embroidery on the peak and an embroidered cap badge. In most navies the peak embroidery identified the rank group of the wearer. The only navies not to have followed this custom were the French and Italian, which shared other uniform features unique to these two countries.

Sailors' dress, or 'square rig', was similar in most navies, although of course there were detailed differences in the collar, scarf and lanyard. The shirt was striped in some navies and plain in others. British sailors received a greatcoat whereas American, Russian and many others had a short peacoat. Rate badges appeared on the sleeve or forearm.

Chief petty officers and some petty officers wore the double-breasted reefer or a single-breasted jacket with a peaked cap; the only navy to combine 'square rig' and peaked cap was the Soviet. Rank was indicated by chevrons or stripes (bars) often combined with a speciality badge. In some navies they wore shoulder straps.

The double-breasted jacket or reefer worn with collar and tie by officers was almost universal, the only two exceptions being the Japanese and Soviet navies. The former retained a rather old-fashioned tunic, which was trimmed with black lace and had a stand collar with rank collar patches. This item of dress had been in use in the US Navy at the turn of the century. Despite efforts to introduce a 'westernized' naval uniform during the Provisional Government, the Soviet Navy reverted to Tsarist traditions and introduced a single-breasted tunic with stiff stand collar and shoulder-boards.

On the reefer, rank distinctions took the form of gold or silver lace rings with a loop for line or executive officers and an emblem for those in other branches. All flag officers in both the Dutch and Portuguese navies shared the same width of ring, and rank was indicated by the number of stars worn above the ring. French admirals also had stars but no lace rings. Shoulder straps were, with a couple of notable exceptions, never worn on the reefer, although Italian and French naval officers had an embroidered passant on both shoulders.

The wearer's branch of service could be identified by the colour that appeared between the rings on the cuff. Officers in the line or executive branches of the German and Soviet navies had a five-pointed star, or, as in the British Royal Navy, the uppermost ring had a loop or curl in it.

Because the white uniforms worn in tropical theatres of operations and the working dress required frequent washing, detachable shoulder straps were found to be most practical, and these came to incorporate rank and branch badges. However, in the Dutch and Turkish navies rank badges on these types of clothing took the form of collar patches.

In the development of naval uniform during World War II one can discern a trend towards restricting the wearing of traditional naval dress to formal or off-duty wear and the gradual militarization of everyday working dress. Combined operations also led to a proliferation of combat tasks performed by naval personnel (other than marines) on land, for which naval uniforms were totally unsuitable. This trend continued after the war and culminated in an experiment by Canada to introduce a standard green uniform for all three branches of her armed forces.

*Uniforms and Insignia of the Navies of World War II* must be welcomed as a vital addition to the library of all those with an interest in maritime history and also by those with a particular interest in uniform and insignia. There is no other publication that covers in such detail the dress, badges of rank and speciality of such a wide range of the nations that, when *JAN1* first appeared, were at war but today are, thankfully, at peace with one another.

Andrew Mollo

London, 1991

# LIST OF PLATES

## ARGENTINE NAVY

| Plate 1 | Commissioned Officers | 1 February 1945 | page 17 |
| Plate 2 | Commissioned Officers, Coast Artillery and Aviation | 1 February 1945 | page 18 |
| Plate 3 | Chief Petty Officers | 1 February 1945 | page 19 |
| Plate 4 | Chief Petty Officers | 1 February 1945 | page 20 |
| Plate 5 | Petty Officers and Seamen | 1 February 1945 | page 21 |
| Plate 6 | Petty Officers and Seamen | 1 February 1945 | page 22 |

The uniform of the Argentine Navy closely resembled that of the British except that only regular line officers had loops on their lace rings, petty officers wore rank badges on the cuffs, and ratings had chevrons on the sleeve. Coastal Artillery and Aviation had an olive green uniform on which the former wore the same rank badges as naval executive officers, and the latter the same rank badges but in black.

## BRAZILIAN NAVY

| Plate 7 | Commissioned Officers | 1 December 1943 | page 23 |
| Plate 8 | Shoulder boards and Sleeve Insignia, Line Officers | 1 December 1943 | page 24 |
| Plate 9 | Petty Officers | 1 December 1943 | page 25 |
| Plate 10 | Petty Officers | 1 December 1943 | page 26 |
| Plate 11 | Seamen | 1 December 1943 | page 27 |
| Plate 12 | Seamen | 1 December 1943 | page 28 |

While officers wore British-style uniforms, ratings more closely resembled US sailors with their white fatigue hats and short 'peacoat'. Petty officers and ratings wore rank badges in the form of chevrons, which were in black on the fatigue uniform.

## BRITISH NAVY

| Plate 13 | Commissioned Officers | December 1944 | page 29 |
| Plate 14 | Shoulder boards and sleeve insignia; line officers | December 1944 | page 30 |
| Plate 15 | Commissioned Officers | January 1944 | page 31 |
| Plate 16 | Corps Colours; Commissioned Officers | December 1944 | page 32 |
| Plate 17 | Petty Officers and Seamen | August 1944 | page 33 |
| Plate 18 | Petty Officers and Seamen | August 1944 | page 34 |
| Plate 19 | Petty Officers and Seamen | August 1944 | page 35 |
| Plate 20 | Petty Officers and Seamen Speciality Insignia | August 1944 | page 36 |
| Plate 21 | Speciality Insignia; Petty Officers and Seamen | August 1944 | page 37 |
| Plate 22 | Speciality Insignia; Petty Officers and Seamen | August 1944 | page 38 |
| Plate 23 | Speciality Insignia; Petty Officers and Seamen | August 1944 | page 39 |
| Plate 24 | Speciality Insignia; Petty Officers and Seamen | August 1944 | page 40 |

In the plates dealing with the British Royal Navy can be found a number of distinctions worn by the navies of the Commonwealth, Dominions and Empire, such as buttons and cap tallies. Five plates are devoted to branch and speciality badges, and these give a good indication of the scope and complexity of this aspect of naval uniform.

## FRENCH NAVY

| | | | |
|---|---|---|---|
| Plate 25 | Commissioned Officers | July 1943 | page 41 |
| Plate 26 | Shoulder Boards and Sleeve Insignia; Line Officers | July 1943 | page 42 |
| Plate 27 | Petty Officers | July 1943 | page 43 |
| Plate 28 | Sleeve Insignia; Petty Officers | July 1943 | page 44 |
| Plate 29 | Seamen | July 1943 | page 45 |
| Plate 30 | Sleeve Insignia; Seamen | July 1943 | page 46 |

Line officers in the French Navy were not, as in most navies, identified by a ring on the rank stripes. Petty officers and ratings wore the same rank insignia as their counterparts in the other branches of the French armed forces.

## GERMAN NAVY

| | | | |
|---|---|---|---|
| Plate 31 | Commissioned, Warrant and 1st Class Petty Officers | February 1943 | page 47 |
| Plate 32 | Shoulder and Sleeve Insignia; Commissioned Officers | February 1943 | page 48 |
| Plate 33 | Petty Officers, 2nd and 3rd Class and Seamen | February 1943 | page 49 |
| Plate 34 | Petty Officers, 2nd and 3rd Class and Seamen | February 1943 | page 50 |
| Plate 35 | Field Gray Uniform; Officers & Men – of Naval Artillery | February 1943 | page 51 |

| | | | |
|---|---|---|---|
| Plate 36 | Field Gray Uniform – Shoulder Insignia, Commissioned Officers | February 1943 | page 52 |
| Plate 37 | Civilian Naval Officials | July 1944 | page 53 |
| Plate 38 | Field Gray and Miscellaneous; Supplement | July 1944 | page 54 |
| Plate 39 | Revision and Addenda | July 1944 | page 55 |
| Plate 40 | Revision and Addenda; Speciality Insignia | July 1944 | page 56 |

On the greatcoat all ranks wore Army-pattern shoulder straps until quite late in the war, when they began to be worn on the reefer. The field-grey uniform, although similar to that worn in the Army, was not identical, having gilt insignia and lace. In 1943 a light khaki tropical was introduced for wear mainly in southern Russia, Italy and the Aegean.

## GREEK NAVY

| | | | |
|---|---|---|---|
| Plate 41 | Officers and Men | February 1945 | page 57 |
| Plate 42 | Shoulder Boards and Sleeve Insignia; Line Officers | February 1945 | page 58 |
| Plate 43 | Speciality Insignia; Commissioned Enlisted Corps Officers, and all Warrant Officers, Petty Officers and Seamen | February 1945 | page 59 |

Greek naval uniform was almost identical to that of the British except that petty officers and ratings wore rank chevrons, while warrant officers had lace rings and chevron on the cuff. On the khaki winter uniform, rank distinction lace was black.

## ITALIAN NAVY

| | | | |
|---|---|---|---|
| Plate 44 | Commissioned Officers | April 1943 | page 60 |

| Plate 45 | Shoulder Insignia | (no date) | page 61 |
| Page 46 | Petty Officers | April 1943 | page 62 |
| Page 47 | Speciality Insignia | April 1943 | page 63 |
| Page 48 | Seamen | April 1943 | page 64 |
| Page 49 | Seamen Speciality Insignia | April 1943 | page 65 |

Italian naval uniform resembled more closely that of France than of Britain, having rank distinction lace on the peaked cap and passants for epaulettes on the reefer. Rank insignia on the cuff corresponded to that in the other branches of the armed forces. Ratings wore chevrons.

## JAPANESE NAVY

| Plate 50 | Commissioned Officers | September 1943 | page 66 |
| Plate 51 | Collar, Shoulder, Sleeve Insignia; Commissioned Officers | September 1943 | page 67 |
| Plate 52 | Commissioned Officers | September 1943 | page 68 |
| Plate 53 | Petty Officers and Seamen | September 1943 | page 69 |
| Plate 54 | Petty Officers and Seamen | September 1943 | page 70 |
| Plate 55 | Special Training Insignia, Old Style; Petty Officers and Seamen | September 1943 | page 71 |
| Plate 56 | Rating Insignia, Old Style; Petty Officers and Seamen | September 1943 | page 72 |

Japanese naval uniform resembled, in some items of dress, that of the United States Navy. In November 1942 new rank insignia for ratings was introduced, and in January 1944 naval officers also adopted the new system of Army rank badges.

## ROYAL NETHERLANDS NAVY

| Plate 57 | Commissioned Officers | October 1943 | page 73 |
| Plate 58 | Shoulder Boards and Sleeve Insignia; Commissioned Officers | October 1943 | page 74 |
| Plate 59 | Warrant and Petty Officers | October 1943 | page 75 |
| Plate 60 | Seamen | October 1943 | page 76 |
| Plate 61 | Speciality Insignia; Warrant and Petty Officers | October 1943 | page 77 |
| Page 62 | Speciality Insignia; Seamen | October 1943 | page 78 |

Apart from the six-pointed stars worn on the cuff by flag officers, Dutch naval uniform conformed to the standard pattern. Missing from this series of plates are those dealing with Marines (Korps Mariniers), who at the beginning of the war wore a grey-green uniform similar to that of the Dutch Army but during the war were equipped with both British and American uniforms.

## PORTUGUESE NAVY

| Plate 63 | Commissioned Officers | June 1943 | page 79 |
| Plate 64 | Petty Officers | June 1943 | page 80 |
| Plate 65 | Seamen | June 1943 | page 81 |

Portuguese naval uniform was not dissimilar to that of the British Royal Navy except that petty officers wore chevrons and ratings wore the American-type fatigue hat.

## RUSSIAN NAVY

| Plate 66 | Commissioned Officers | February 1945 | page 82 |
| Plate 67 | Shoulder Boards and Sleeve Insignia; Line Officers | February 1945 | page 83 |
| Plate 68 | Warrant Officers, Petty Officers and Seamen | February 1945 | page 84 |
| Plate 69 | Warrant Officers, Petty Officers and Seamen | February 1945 | page 85 |

Plate 70    Warrant Officers, Petty Officers and
            Seamen                          February 1945        page 86

The Soviet Navy went to war in June 1941 wearing the rank insignia introduced in December 1935. All ranks wore their badges of rank on the cuff, even on the greatcoat and peacoat. Traditional shoulder-boards were re-introduced in January 1943, and henceforth rank distinction lace on the cuff was only retained by line or executive officers. There was no special uniform for marines or shore-based naval personnel.

## SPANISH NAVY

Plate 71    Commissioned officers              March 1943           page 87
Plate 72    Warrant Officer, Chief and First
            Class Petty Officer               March 1943           page 88
Plate 73    Petty Officers, 2nd and 3rd Class,
            and Seamen                        March 1943           page 89

The uniform illustrated in these plates continued to be worn until the death of Generalissimo Francisco Franco. Not illustrated is the gorget worn by duty officers, which as far as I know, is the last example of this particular item of uniform still in use to this day.

## SWEDISH NAVY

Plate 74    Coast Artillery; Officers and Men     June 1945        page 90
Plate 75    Officers and Men                      June 1945        page 91

As in the Portuguese Navy, flag rank was denoted by stars on the cuff. Ratings wore rank badges on the sleeve. The Coast Artillery had an army-style grey uniform and used army rank titles.

## TURKISH NAVY

Plate 76    Commissioned Officers             August 1943          page 92
Plate 77    Petty Officers and Seamen         August 1943          page 93

An unusual detail of Turkish naval uniform was the extensive use of collar patches in corps colours on which appeared speciality emblems for most branches but excluding line. Naval officers serving on land could wear an army-style uniform with army badges of rank.

## UNITED STATES NAVY

Plate 78    Navy Caps and Cap Devices                              page 94
Plate 79    Navy Badges                                            page 95
Plate 80    Navy Enlisted Men's and Nurses' White Uniform Caps     page 96
Plate 81    Navy Speciality Marks                                  page 97
Plate 82    Navy Specialist Ratings                                page 98
Plate 83    Navy Buttons                                           page 99
Plate 84    Marine Corps Collar, Lapel and Shoulder Strap
            Insignia                                               page 100
Plate 85    Marine Corps Chevrons and Service Stripes              page 101
Plate 86    Marine Corps Aviation Badges                           page 102
Plate 87    Coast Guard Cap Insignia                               page 103
Plate 88    Coast Guard Speciality Marks                           page 104
Plate 89    Navy Aircraft Insignia                                 page 105
Plate 90    Navy and Marine Corps Aircraft Insignia                page 106

### Decorations and Medals

Plate 91    Decorations, Medals & Ribbons Authorised During
            World War II                                           page 107
Plate 92    Navy and Marine Corps Decorations                      page 108
Plate 93    Navy, Marine Corps and Coast Guard Medals              page 109
Plate 94    Navy Service Ribbons for Decorations and Medals        page 110
Plate 95    Marine Corps Marksmanship Badges                       page 111
Plate 96    Navy Gunnery and Marksmanship Badges                   page 112

PLATE 1

# COMMISSIONED OFFICERS

# ARGENTINE NAVY

**CAPTAIN, LINE**
Capitán de Navío
(Blue service uniform)

**CAP INSIGNIA**
All Commissioned Officers
(Red background, Coast Artillery; olive green
background with Aviation uniform)

## AVIATION INSIGNIA
Worn on left breast

**NAVAL PILOT**
Piloto Aviador Naval

**SEAPLANE PILOT**
Piloto de Hidroaviones

**AIR PERSONNEL**
Personal Aeronáutico
(Worn by officers not qualified as pilots)

**LIEUTENANT, LINE**
Teniente de Fragata
(White service uniform)

## CORPS COLORS

Worn between stripes, on sleeve and shoulder
board. If only one stripe, the color appears on
both sides of the stripe. Line (which includes
Aviation and Coast Artillery) has no Corps color.

**ENGINEERING**
Ingenieros

**MEDICAL**
Sanidad

**SUPPLY**
Administración

**LEGAL**
Jurídico

**SUBMARINE SERVICE**
Servicio en submarinos
(Worn on left breast)

**BUTTON**
All personnel

**ENSIGN, LINE**
Alférez de Fragata
(Fatigue uniform)

J.A.N. No. 1, February, 1945   DIVISION OF NAVAL INTELLIGENCE

# PLATE 2

## COMMISSIONED OFFICERS
### COAST ARTILLERY AND AVIATION

**SHOULDER BOARDS AND SLEEVE STRIPES; LINE**

NOTE: Commander wears same cap as Lieutenant Commander.

| ADMIRAL | VICE ADMIRAL | REAR ADMIRAL | CAPTAIN | COMMANDER |
|---|---|---|---|---|
| Almirante | Vicealmirante | Contraalmirante | Capitán de Navío | Capitán de Fragata |

#### COAST ARTILLERY CAP
Visor braid for Major and Lieutenant Colonel. Colonel and General wear same visor braid as Navy Captain and Admiral.

#### COAST ARTILLERY OVERSEAS CAP
All ranks. No insignia worn.

### COAST ARTILLERY
This Corps maintains coastal defenses; and in other respects it is similar to U. S. Marine Corps. Rank Insignia same as Navy, but Army titles are used.

### AVIATION UNIFORM
In addition to regular Navy uniforms, Aviation Officers may wear uniform at right. Breeches and black leggings permitted. Regular Navy sleeve stripes worn in black. Cap is olive green with regular Navy Insignia.

### COAST ARTILLERY AND AVIATION SHOULDER STRAPS
Note: Red piping for Coast Artillery only.

NOTE: All regular naval officers (Line and Corps) wear loop on top stripe of sleeve and shoulder board. Reserve Officers, Civilian Naval Officials, and Chaplains do not wear the loop.

NOTE: Coast Artillery uniform has gold sleeve stripes as illustrated. The Aviation olive green uniform has black sleeve stripes similarly arranged.

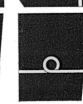

| LIEUTENANT COMMANDER | LIEUTENANT | LIEUTENANT (jg) | ENSIGN | SUB-ENSIGN |
|---|---|---|---|---|
| Teniente de Navío | Teniente de Fragata | Alférez de Navío | Alférez de. Fragata | Guardiamarina |

**MAJOR, COAST ARTILLERY**
Mayor, Artillería de Costas
(Service uniform. Breeches and black leggings also worn)

General and Colonel (Coast Artillery)

Commander and Lieutenant Commander (Aviation); Lieutenant Colonel and Major (Coast Artillery)

Lieutenant and below (Aviation); Captain and below (Coast Artillery)

**LIEUTENANT (jg), AVIATION**
Alférez de Navío, Aeronáutico
(Service uniform; see description at left)

J.A.N. No. 1
February, 1945
DIVISION OF NAVAL INTELLIGENCE

**PLATE 3**

# CHIEF PETTY OFFICERS

## ARGENTINE NAVY

CAP INSIGNIA; CPO, 1st AND 2nd CLASS

CAP INSIGNIA; CPO, 3rd AND 4th CLASS

**RATING INSIGNIA; CPO, 1st AND 2nd CLASS**
Worn on both lower sleeves. Color is gold except for Aviation olive green uniform where it is black.

CHIEF PETTY OFFICER
1st CLASS, SIGNALMAN
Suboficial Mayor, Señalero

CHIEF PETTY OFFICER
2th CLASS, TORPEDOMAN
Suboficial Principal,
Torpedista,

**RATING INSIGNIA; CPO, 3rd AND 4th CLASS**
Worn on both sleeves between elbow and shoulder. Color is gold except for Aviation olive green uniform where it is black.

CHIEF PETTY OFFICER
3rd CLASS, TORPEDOMAN
Suboficial Primero,
Torpedista

CHIEF PETTY OFFICER
4th CLASS, ELECTRICIAN
Suboficial Segundo,
Electricista

NAVAL AIR PILOT
Piloto Aviador Naval
(Worn on left breast)

SEAPLANE PILOT
Piloto de Hidroaviones
(Worn on left breast)

SUBMARINE PERSONNEL
Personal de submarinos
(Worn on left breast)

BUTTON
All personnel

CHIEF PETTY OFFICER 1st CLASS, SIGNALMAN
Suboficial Mayor, Señalero
(Blue service uniform)

CHIEF PETTY OFFICER 3rd CLASS, TORPEDOMAN
Suboficial Primero, Torpedista
(White service uniform)

CHIEF PETTY OFFICER 4th CLASS, ELECTRICIAN
Suboficial Segundo, Electricista
(Fatigue uniform)

J.A.N. No. 1, February, 1945   DIVISION OF NAVAL INTELLIGENCE

PLATE 4

# CHIEF PETTY OFFICERS

**SPECIALTY INSIGNIA**—Worn above Rating Insignia. Same colors as Rating Insignia.

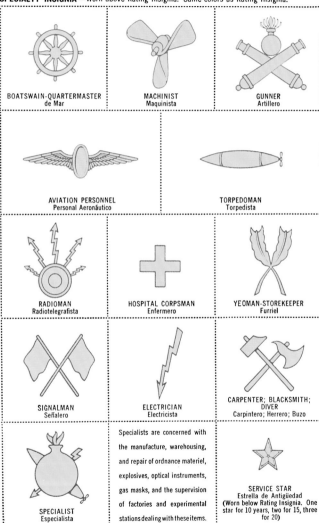

BOATSWAIN-QUARTERMASTER
de Mar

MACHINIST
Maquinista

GUNNER
Artillero

AVIATION PERSONNEL
Personal Aeronáutico

TORPEDOMAN
Torpedista

RADIOMAN
Radiotelegrafista

HOSPITAL CORPSMAN
Enfermero

YEOMAN-STOREKEEPER
Furriel

SIGNALMAN
Señalero

ELECTRICIAN
Electricista

CARPENTER; BLACKSMITH;
DIVER
Carpintero; Herrero; Buzo

SPECIALIST
Especialista

Specialists are concerned with the manufacture, warehousing, and repair of ordnance materiel, explosives, optical instruments, gas masks, and the supervision of factories and experimental stations dealing with these items.

SERVICE STAR
Estrella de Antigüedad
(Worn below Rating Insignia. One star for 10 years, two for 15, three for 20)

J.A.N. No. 1
February, 1945
DIVISION OF NAVAL
INTELLIGENCE

# COAST ARTILLERY AND AVIATION

(Coast Artillery maintains coastal defenses; in other respects it is similar to U.S. Marines)

SERGEANT MAJOR 1st CLASS,
COAST ARTILLERY
Suboficial Mayor, Defensa de Costas
(Rating Insignia same as regular Navy)

**COAST ARTILLERY CAP**
Cap insignia is same as that worn by equivalent rank in regular Navy.

**COAST ARTILLERY OVERSEAS CAP**
All ranks. No insignia worn.

## AVIATION UNIFORM

In addition to regular Navy uniforms and insignia, Aviation CPO may wear the uniform illustrated at right. Rating Insignia is same as Navy but in black. Cap is olive green with regular Navy insignia.

## COAST ARTILLERY; SPECIAL INSIGNIA

Worn above Rating Insignia unless otherwise noted.

NAVAL INFANTRY
Infantería de Marina

SERVICE STAR
Estrella de Antigüedad
(Worn below Rating Insignia. One star for 10 years, two for 15, three for 20)

YEOMAN
Oficinista Naval

MUSICIAN
Músico

DRUMMERS AND
BUGLERS
Banda Lisa

# ARGENTINE NAVY

CHIEF PETTY OFFICER 4th CLASS,
AVIATION
Suboficial Segundo, Aeronáutico
(See description at left)

**PLATE 5**

# PETTY OFFICERS 1st, 2nd, 3rd CLASS AND SEAMEN

**ARGENTINE NAVY**

**PETTY OFFICER 1st CLASS, SIGNALMAN**
Cabo Principal, Señalero
(White dress uniform)

**NAVAL BADGE**
Distintivo de Marina de Guerra
(For all personnel below CPO. Worn on both upper sleeves, on dress uniforms only, above all other insignia. Colors: gold on blue uniform, blue on white uniform)

## RATING INSIGNIA

For PO 1st, 2nd, 3rd Class. Seamen have no Rating Insignia. Worn on both upper sleeves, below Specialty Insignia. Gold for blue dress; red for blue undress; blue for white dress and undress.

**PETTY OFFICER, 1st CLASS**
Cabo Principal

**PETTY OFFICER, 2nd CLASS**
Cabo Primero

**PETTY OFFICER, 3rd CLASS**
Cabo Segundo

**PETTY OFFICER 2nd CLASS, TORPEDOMAN**
Cabo Primero, Torpedista
(Blue dress uniform)

**DRESS CAP**
For PO 1st, 2nd, 3rd Class and Seamen. Cap bands have A.R.A. (Armada República Argentina) plus ship or station.

## SPECIAL SERVICE INSIGNIA
Worn on left breast.

**NAVAL AIR PILOT**
Piloto Aviador Naval

**SEAPLANE PILOT**
Piloto de Hidroaviones

**SUBMARINE PERSONNEL**
Personal de submarinos

**BUTTON**
Worn on dress overcoat and on
Coast Artillery uniform

**SEAMAN 1st CLASS, HOSPITAL CORPSMAN**
Marinero Primero, Enfermero
(White undress uniform)

**PLATE 6**

## PETTY OFFICERS 1st, 2nd, 3rd CLASS AND SEAMEN

**ARGENTINE NAVY**

BOATSWAIN-
QUARTERMASTER
de Mar

### SPECIALTY INSIGNIA
Worn on both upper sleeves, immediately above Rating Insignia. Colors: gold for blue dress uniform; red for blue undress uniform; blue for white dress and undress uniforms. Seaman, 1st Class, wears Specialty Insignia but no Rating Insignia. Seaman, 2nd Class, and Apprentice wear no insignia whatsoever, except the Naval Badge on dress uniforms.

GUNNER
Artillero

SIGNALMAN
Señalero

RADIOMAN
Radiotelegrafista

ELECTRICIAN
Electricista

MACHINIST
Maquinista

YEOMAN-STOREKEEPER
Furriel

AVIATION PERSONNEL
Personal Aeronáutico

PAINTER
Pintor

TORPEDOMAN
Torpedista

COOK; BAKER
Cocinero; Panadero

LAUNDERER
Lavandero

STEWARD
Camarero

BARBER
Peluquero

TAILOR
Sastre

HOSPITAL CORPSMAN
Enfermero

CARPENTER; BLACKSMITH; DIVER; METALSMITH; PLUMBER
Carpintero; Herrero; Buzo; Hojalatero; Plomero

Specialists are concerned with the manufacture, warehousing, and repair of ordnance materiel, explosives, optical instruments, gas masks, and the supervision of factories and experimental stations dealing with these items.

SPECIALIST
Especialista

SERVICE STAR
Estrella de Antigüedad
(Worn below Rating Insignia. One star for 10 years, two for 15, three for 20)

### COAST ARTILLERY
(Maintains coastal defenses and performs duties similar to U. S. Marines)

### COAST ARTILLERY; RATING INSIGNIA
Chevrons and position are same as equivalent grades in Navy, but color is red. Worn only by grades equivalent to PO 1st, 2nd, 3rd Class.

COAST ARTILLERY CAP
Worn by all grades below equivalent of CPO. Green overseas cap may also be worn.

### COAST ARTILLERY; SPECIAL INSIGNIA
Worn on both upper sleeves, above Rating Insignia, by all except equivalents of Seaman, 2nd Class, and Apprentice.

NAVAL INFANTRY
Infantería de Marina

SERVICE STAR
Estrella de Antigüedad
(Worn below Rating Insignia. One star for 10 years, two for 15, three for 20)

YEOMAN
Oficinista Naval

MUSICIAN
Músico

DRUMMERS AND BUGLERS
Banda Lisa

SERGEANT, COAST ARTILLERY
Cabo Segundo de Defensa de Costas
(Ordinary trousers may also be worn)

## PLATE 7

## COMMISSIONED OFFICERS

## BRAZILIAN NAVY

**CAPTAIN, LINE**
Capitão de Mar e Guerra
(Submarine Service)

### CORPS INSIGNIA

Corps Officers are distinguished by insignia, illustrated below, worn above the top stripe of sleeve and shoulder board; no loop is worn on top stripe, except where specifically noted.

DOCTORS
Médicos

CHEMISTS
Químicos

DENTISTS
Dentistas

PHARMACISTS
Farmacêuticos

SUPPLY
Intendentes Navais

ACCOUNTS
Contadores Navais

ENGINEERS
Engenheiros Navais

NAVAL ACADEMY PROFESSORS
Lentes da Escola Naval

Note: Engineers and Professors wear loop like Line Officers. Their Corps insignia is worn above the loop of the sleeve stripe and superimposed on the anchor of the shoulder board.

**LIEUTENANT COMMANDER, LINE**
Capitão de Corveta

BUTTON

RIVER AND COASTAL PILOT
Prático
(Worn as a regular Corps insignia by former civilian pilots. Restricted to rank of Ensign)

CAP INSIGNIA
All Commissioned Officers

SUBMARINE INSIGNIA
Worn on left breast

HONORARY OFFICER (COMMANDER)
Oficial Honorário
(May rank from Captain to Ensign)

Sleeve

Shoulder Board

**ENSIGN, LINE**
Segundo Tenente
(Fatigue uniform)

## PLATE 8

# SHOULDER BOARDS AND SLEEVE INSIGNIA; LINE OFFICERS

**BRAZILIAN NAVY**

| ADMIRAL<br>Almirante | VICE ADMIRAL<br>Vice-Almirante | REAR ADMIRAL<br>Contra-Almirante | CAPTAIN<br>Capitão de Mar e Guerra | COMMANDER<br>Capitão de Fragata | LIEUTENANT COMMANDER<br>Capitão de Corveta | LIEUTENANT<br>Capitão-Tenente | LIEUTENANT (jg)<br>Primeiro Tenente | ENSIGN<br>Segundo Tenente | PROBATIONARY ENSIGN<br>Guarda-Marinha |

## SPECIALTY INSIGNIA; AUXILIARY OFFICERS' CORPS

These men form a Corps of Officers commissioned from the ranks, and they wear their Specialty Insignia in gold above stripes on sleeve and shoulder board. No loop is worn. Their duties are similar to U.S. Warrant Officers. They may hold rank from Lieutenant Commander to Ensign

| TORPEDOMAN<br>Oficial Auxiliar de Torpedos | BOATSWAIN SERVICE<br>Oficial Auxiliar de Manobra | CARPENTER<br>Oficial Auxiliar de Carpintaria | GUNNER<br>Oficial Auxiliar de Artilharia | SIGNALMAN-QUARTERMASTER<br>Oficial Auxiliar de Sinais | RADIOMAN<br>Oficial Auxiliar de Rádio | YEOMAN-STOREKEEPER<br>Oficial Auxiliar de Escrita |

| MOTOR MACHINIST<br>Oficial Auxiliar de Motores e Máquinas Especiais | BOILERMAKER-WATER TENDER<br>Oficial Auxiliar de Caldeiras e suas Máquinas Auxiliares | ELECTRICIAN<br>Oficial Auxiliar de Eletricidade | MACHINE TOOL OPERATOR<br>Oficial Auxiliar Torneiro-Frezador | MACHINIST<br>Oficial Auxiliar de Máquinas Principais | COPPERSMITH<br>Oficial Auxiliar Caldeireiro de Cobre-Soldador | MEDICAL SERVICE<br>Oficial Auxiliar de Sáude | ATHLETIC INSTRUCTOR<br>Oficial Auxiliar de Educacão Física | BLACKSMITH<br>Oficial Auxiliar Ferreiro-Serralheiro |

J.A.N.No. 1:
DECEMBER 1943

**PLATE 9**

**PETTY OFFICERS**

CHIEF PETTY OFFICER, MACHINIST
Sub-oficial Condutor de Máquinas
(Blue dress uniform)

CAP INSIGNIA
Chief Petty Officers

BUTTON
All Petty Officers

**RATING INSIGNIA; CHIEF PETTY OFFICER**
Worn on shoulder boards for blue service and white uniforms, otherwise on both cuffs. Anchor and Specialty Insignia in black for fatigue uniform.

Sleeve          Shoulder Board

CHIEF PETTY OFFICER, YEOMAN
Sub-oficial Escrevente
(White service uniform)

CHIEF PETTY OFFICER, GUNNER
Sub-oficial Artilheiro
(Blue service uniform)

CAP INSIGNIA
P.O. 1st, 2nd, and 3rd Class

**RATING INSIGNIA; P.O. 1st, 2nd, and 3rd CLASS**
Worn on both upper sleeves. In gold for white and blue uniforms; in black for fatigue uniform.

PETTY OFFICER 1st CLASS, MACHINIST
Primeiro Sargento Condutor de Máquinas

PETTY OFFICER 2nd CLASS, YEOMAN
Segundo Sargento Escrevente

PETTY OFFICER 3rd CLASS, GUNNER
Terceiro Sargento Artilheiro

PETTY OFFICER 1st CLASS, MACHINIST
Primeiro Sargento Condutor de Máquinas
(White service uniform)

## PLATE 10

# PETTY OFFICERS

# BRAZILIAN NAVY

**PETTY OFFICER 2nd CLASS, YEOMAN**
Segundo Sargento Escrevente
(Blue service uniform)

## SPECIALTY INSIGNIA — ALL PETTY OFFICERS

These insignia are in gold for the blue and white uniforms; they are embroidered in black for the fatigue uniform. They are worn immediately below the anchor by Chief Petty Officers. All other Petty Officers wear their Specialty Insignia immediately above the vertex of their rating chevrons.

**TORPEDOMAN**
Torpedista

**BOATSWAIN**
Manobra
(C.P.O. is called Contra-mestre)

**CARPENTER**
Carpinteiro

**COPPERSMITH**
Caldeireiro de Cobre-Soldador

**SIGNALMAN-QUARTERMASTER**
Sinaleiro

**ATHLETIC INSTRUCTOR**
Monitor de Educação Física

**GUNNER**
Artilheiro

**BLACKSMITH**
Ferreiro-Serralheiro

**HOSPITAL CORPSMAN**
Enfermeiro

**YEOMAN-STOREKEEPER**
Escrevente

**RIVER AND COASTAL PILOT**
Prático

**MACHINIST**
Condutor de Máquinas

**BOILERMAKER-WATER TENDER**
Condutor de Caldeiras

**ELECTRICIAN**
Eletricista

**MOTOR MACHINIST**
Motorista

**MACHINE TOOL OPERATOR**
Torneiro-Frezador

**RADIOMAN**
Rádio-Telegrafista

**PETTY OFFICER 3rd CLASS, GUNNER**
Terceiro Sargento Artilheiro
(Fatigue uniform)

J.A.N. No. 1:
DECEMBER 1943

PLATE 11

**SEAMEN**

**BRAZILIAN NAVY**

DRESS CAP

MARINHA DO BRASIL

CAP BAND FOR SEAMEN

APRENDIZ MARINHEIRO

CAP BAND FOR APPRENTICE SEAMAN

UNDRESS AND FATIGUE CAP

### RATING INSIGNIA
Red for blue uniforms and overcoat; blue for
white uniform; black for fatigue uniform.

LEADING SEAMAN, MACHINIST
Cabo Condutor de Máquinas
(Blue dress uniform)

SEAMAN 1st CLASS, YEOMAN
Marinheiro 1a Classe Escrevente
(White dress uniform)

LEADING SEAMAN,
MACHINIST
Cabo Condutor de Máquinas
(On both upper sleeves)

SEAMAN 1st CLASS,
YEOMAN
Marinheiro 1a Classe
Escrevente
(On upper left sleeve only)

SEAMAN 2nd CLASS,
GUNNER
Marinheiro 2a Classe Artilheiro
(On upper left sleeve only)

SEAMAN 2nd CLASS, GUNNER
Marinheiro 2a Classe Artilheiro
(Blue undress uniform)

SEAMAN, 2nd CLASS
Marinheiro 2a Classe
(Fatigue uniform; Specialty Insignia
never worn)

J.A.N. No. 1: DECEMBER 1943

PLATE 12

## SEAMEN

**SEAMAN 1st CLASS, MACHINIST**
Marinheiro 1a Classe Condutor de Máquinas
(Overcoat with fatigue uniform)

J.A.N. No. 1
DECEMBER 1943

### SPECIALTY INSIGNIA

These insignia are worn immediately above the vertex of the rating chevrons on all uniforms with the exception of the fatigue uniform, where the rating chevrons alone are worn. Apprentice Seamen, having no rating chevrons, do not wear any Specialty Insignia. The colors of the insignia are as follows: red for blue uniforms and overcoat, blue for white uniforms.

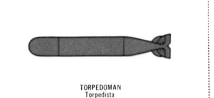

**TORPEDOMAN**
Torpedista

**CARPENTER**
Carpinteiro

**GUNNER**
Artilheiro

**SIGNALMAN-QUARTERMASTER**
Sinaleiro

**BOATSWAIN SERVICE**
Manobra

**MACHINIST**
Condutor de Máquinas

**ELECTRICIAN**
Eletricista

**RADIOMAN**
Rádio-Telegrafista

**YEOMAN-STOREKEEPER**
Escrevente

### SPECIAL SERVICE INSIGNIA

The Good Conduct star is worn above all other sleeve insignia. The Gun Aimer award is worn above the Specialty Insignia. The Conscript bar is worn like any ordinary Specialty Insignia

**GOOD CONDUCT STAR**
Estrela de Comportamento

**GUN AIMER, GROUP AWARD**
Grupo de Pontaria

**CONSCRIPT**
Conscrito

### BRAZILIAN NAVY

## MESSMEN SERVICE

Cap like P.O.'s but with insignia shown below. Uniforms (white, blue, and fatigue) similar to P.O. fatigue uniform but with hooked, turned-down collar. Collar tabs have anchors same color as sleeve stripes.

CAP INSIGNIA FOR MESSMEN

## MESSMEN INSIGNIA

Markings above vertex of rating chevrons indicate specialty. Colors same as for Seamen insignia. Worn on both upper sleeves by 1st Class Messman rating, on upper left sleeve by lower ratings.

**STEWARD, 1st CLASS**
Taifeiro-Arrumador 1a Classe
(Ranks with Leading Seaman)

**COOK, 2nd CLASS**
Cozinheiro 2a Classe
(Ranks with Seaman, 1st Class)

**BARBER, 3rd CLASS**
Barbeiro 3a Classe
(Ranks with Seaman, 2nd Class)

**BAKER, 3rd CLASS**
Padeiro 3a Classe
(Ranks with Seaman, 2nd Class)

PLATE 13

**COMMISSIONED OFFICERS**

**BRITISH NAVY**

TROPICAL HELMET

The commissioned personnel pictured herein all appear as Line Officers (British: Executive Officers), Royal Navy. Officers of the Royal Navy, Royal Naval Reserve and Royal Naval Volunteer Reserve are differentiated only by the form of their rank stripes. Corps Officers, as opposed to Line Officers, are distinguished by Corps colors which appear between the rank stripes on sleeves and shoulder boards.

STEEL HELMET
Same as Army helmet

CAP INSIGNIA
All Commissioned Officers

COMBINED OPERATIONS INSIGNIA
On both shoulders of Army-type battle dress; on right cuff of usual Navy uniforms.

| ADMIRAL OF THE FLEET | ADMIRAL | VICE ADMIRAL | REAR ADMIRAL | COMMODORE, FIRST CLASS |

COMMODORE SECOND CLASS,
ROYAL NAVY
Blue service uniform. White cap
permitted on occasion.

CAP, SHOULDER BOARDS, AND SLEEVE INSIGNIA FOR FLAG OFFICERS, ROYAL NAVY

COMMANDER, ROYAL NAVY
White service uniform.

J.A.N. No. 1: JANUARY 1944

PLATE 14

**SHOULDER BOARDS AND
SLEEVE INSIGNIA;
LINE OFFICERS**

**BRITISH NAVY**

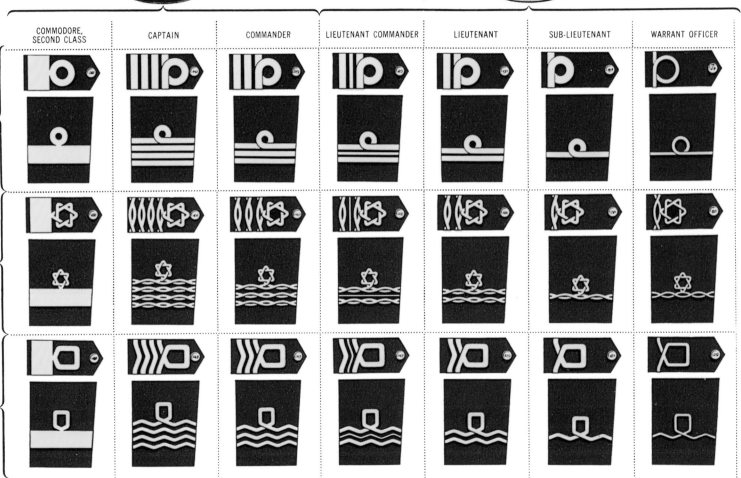

|  | COMMODORE, SECOND CLASS | CAPTAIN | COMMANDER | LIEUTENANT COMMANDER | LIEUTENANT | SUB-LIEUTENANT | WARRANT OFFICER |
|---|---|---|---|---|---|---|---|

**RN (ROYAL NAVY)**
Made up of professional naval personnel and former professionals recalled to active duty. Higher ranks, which exist only for Royal Navy, are shown on page at left.

**RNR (ROYAL NAVAL RESERVE)**
Composed chiefly of men who in private life were merchant marine officers or were otherwise closely connected with maritime affairs.

**RNVR (ROYAL NAVAL VOLUNTEER RESERVE)**
Composed of men of varying professional backgrounds.

J.A.N. No. 1
December, 1944
DIVISION OF NAVAL
INTELLIGENCE

# PLATE 15

## COMMISSIONED OFFICERS

**BRITISH NAVY**

**LIEUTENANT COMMANDER, ROYAL NAVY**
Khaki service uniform.

**LIEUTENANT, ROYAL NAVY**
Tropical uniform.

### BUTTONS

COMMODORE 1st CLASS AND ABOVE, ROYAL NAVY

COMMODORE 2nd CLASS AND BELOW, ROYAL NAVY

ROYAL CANADIAN NAVY

ROYAL AUSTRALIAN NAVY

ROYAL INDIAN NAVY

SOUTH AFRICAN NAVAL FORCES

### SOUTH AFRICA, DISTINGUISHING MARKS
(Illustrated for Sub-Lieutenant)

   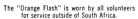

Sleeve　　　　Shoulder Board

The "Orange Flash" is worn by all volunteers for service outside of South Africa.

**SUB-LIEUTENANT, ROYAL NAVY**
Blue working uniform.

**SUB-LIEUTENANT, ROYAL NAVY**
Army-type battle dress, worn ashore in Combined Operations

PLATE 16

## CORPS COLORS; COMMISSIONED OFFICERS

BRITISH NAVY

| ORDNANCE | ENGINEER | ELECTRICAL; ELECTRICAL ENGINEER | SHIPWRIGHT; NAVAL CONSTRUCTOR | MEDICAL | DENTAL | WARDMASTER | SUPPLY AND SECRETARIAT | INSTRUCTOR; SCHOOLMASTER | SPECIAL BRANCH RNVR only |

## SHOULDER BOARDS AND SLEEVE INSIGNIA; CORPS

AIR BRANCH INSIGNIA

| VICE ADMIRAL, RN Medical | REAR ADMIRAL, RN Supply and Secretariat | CAPTAIN, RN Dental | COMMANDER, RNR Supply and Secretariat | LIEUTENANT COMMANDER, RNR Medical | LIEUTENANT, RNVR Instructor | SUB-LIEUTENANT, RNVR Special Branch |

PILOT
Left arm above loop for blue uniform; left breast for white and khaki uniforms.

## MIDSHIPMEN AND CADETS, LINE; COLLAR INSIGNIA

| MIDSHIPMAN, RN | MIDSHIPMAN, RNR | MIDSHIPMAN, RNVR | CADET, RN | CADET, RNR | CADET, RNVR |

Midshipmen and Cadets of the Line in service dress are distinguished solely by collar insignia; but those of the Corps wear a single narrow stripe of Corps color, without loop, on sleeves or shoulder boards, in addition to the standard collar insignia here illustrated.

OBSERVER
Worn in same position as Pilot insignia.

## WOMEN'S ROYAL NAVAL SERVICE ("WRENS"); HAT, SLEEVE AND SHOULDER INSIGNIA

| HAT INSIGNIA Gold wreath for Medical Officers | SUPERINTENDENT Ranks with Captain | CHIEF OFFICER Ranks with Commander | FIRST OFFICER Ranks with Lieutenant Commander | SECOND OFFICER Ranks with Lieutenant | THIRD OFFICER Ranks with Sub-Lieutenant |

Director and Deputy Director wear stripes of Rear Admiral and Commodore 2nd Class respectively, in blue. Medical Officers wear RNVR gold stripes, red Corps color, gold cap insignia.

SUB-LIEUTENANT, RN, AIR BRANCH
RN and RNVR Officers who enter Navy directly into Air Branch wear "A" in loop of sleeve and shoulder board, while transfers to Air Branch from other Branches or Corps omit the "A."

J.A.N. No. 1
December, 1944
DIVISION OF NAVAL INTELLIGENCE

PLATE 17

**PETTY OFFICERS AND SEAMEN**

**BRITISH NAVY**

CHIEF PETTY OFFICER,
GUNNER'S MATE
Blue dress uniform

CHIEF PETTY OFFICER,
VISUAL SIGNALMAN 2nd CLASS
(Chief Yeoman of Signals)
Blue service uniform. White cap permitted
with all blue uniforms here illustrated.

PETTY OFFICER, STOKER
Good Conduct chevron. Double breasted
jacket with gold insignia for dress wear.

PETTY OFFICER (UNCONFIRMED),
WIRELESS TELEGRAPHIST
1st CLASS
Good Conduct chevrons. Gold insignia for
dress wear. After 1 year as PO, Seaman
dress is changed to regular PO jacket.

MISCELLANEOUS JUNIOR RATING,
WRITER
Uniform for all below PO except men in
Seaman, Sailmaker, Signal, Teleg., Coder,
Photog., Wireman, Stoker, Naval Airman,
Observer and Air Gunner, Rating Pilot, and
Air Mech. Branches.

J.A.N. NO. 1: AUGUST 1944.   DIVISION OF NAVAL INTELLIGENCE

**PLATE 18**

**PETTY OFFICERS AND SEAMEN**

**BRITISH NAVY**

### CAP BANDS FOR SEAMEN
Officer Candidates wear solid white cap band.

| | |
|---|---|
| **H.M.S.** | **H.M.C.S.** |
| ROYAL NAVY | ROYAL CANADIAN NAVY |
| **H.M.A.S.** | **H.M.N.Z.S.** |
| ROYAL AUSTRALIAN NAVY | ROYAL NEW ZEALAND NAVY |
| **H.M.I.S.** | **S. & A.** |
| ROYAL INDIAN NAVY | SOUTH AFRICAN NAVAL FORCES |

### ARM BANDS

**GUARD DUTY**
Worn on overcoat.

**N** P

**NAVAL POLICE**

BUTTON, FOR CPO AND PO

**CHIEF PETTY OFFICER,
MASTER-AT-ARMS**
White service uniform.
Specialty insignia often omitted.

**PETTY OFFICER,
GUNNER'S MATE**
Good Conduct chevrons.
White service uniform.

**LEADING SEAMAN,
LEADING TORPEDOMAN**
Good Conduct chevrons.
White service uniform.
Work jumper is white throughout.

**MISCELLANEOUS JUNIOR
RATING, ARTISAN 5th
CLASS**
White service uniform.

J.A.N. NO. 1:
AUGUST 1944
DIVISION OF
NAVAL
INTELLIGENCE

**PLATE 19**

**PETTY OFFICERS AND SEAMEN**

**BRITISH NAVY**

**CHIEF PETTY OFFICER**
Tropical uniform.
PO differs only by having PO rating insignia
on left arm and PO cap badge.

**LEADING SEAMAN**
Tropical shore-going uniform.
H.M.S. capband also may be worn.
White shoes, blue belt for shipboard wear.

**MISCELLANEOUS JUNIOR RATING**
Tropical shore-going uniform.
White shoes, blue belt for shipboard wear.

**PETTY OFFICER**
Tropical landing uniform

**SEAMAN**
Summer landing uniform.
Army battle dress also worn.

J.A.N.NO.1: AUGUST 1944.   DIVISION OF NAVAL INTELLIGENCE

**PLATE 20**

# PETTY OFFICERS AND SEAMEN

# SPECIALTY INSIGNIA

# BRITISH NAVY

## RATING INSIGNIA

POs and Leading Seamen: gold on blue dress uniform, red on blue service uniform, blue on white uniform. Able Seamen and below wear no rating insignia.

**CHIEF PETTY OFFICER**
Both sleeves, blue or white uniform.

**PETTY OFFICER**
Upper left sleeve.

**LEADING SEAMAN**
Upper left sleeve.

## GOOD CONDUCT CHEVRONS
Colors same as Rating Insignia. Not worn by CPO.

**FOR 13 OR MORE YEARS.**
Upper left sleeve.

**FOR 8 YEARS.**
Upper left sleeve.

**FOR 3 YEARS.**
Upper left sleeve.

## CAP INSIGNIA

**CHIEF PETTY OFFICER**

**PETTY OFFICER**

**MISCELLANEOUS JUNIOR RATING**

## SUN-HELMET INSIGNIA

J.A.N. NO. 1:
AUGUST 1944
DIVISION OF
NAVAL
INTELLIGENCE

**CHIEF PETTY OFFICER**

**PETTY OFFICER**

**MISCELLANEOUS JUNIOR RATING**

CPO: Worn above the lapels, in gold for blue dress uniform, in red for blue service uniform; on lower right sleeve in gold for white uniform. Sick Berth and other medical specialists wear insignia on upper right sleeve only, on both blue and white uniforms.

PO and Seaman: Upper right sleeve; gold for blue dress, red for blue service, blue for white uniform.

WRENS' insignia is blue for all uniforms.

In British naval practice, specialty and rating are generally unrelated. A man may have a high status in a specialty without advancing beyond a seaman's rating; or he may be a CPO but still not be highly qualified in his particular specialty. In such cases, advancement in rating would depend on leadership, education, etc. The newer branches, such as Aviation, tend to associate rating and specialty more closely, similar to U. S. naval practice.

LEGEND: 1 = CPO; 2 = PO; 3 = Leading Seaman or equivalent; 4 = Able Seaman or equivalent; 5 = Ordinary Seaman or equivalent; 6 = Boy.

**VISUAL SIGNALMAN, 1st CLASS**
Open to: 1, 2, 3

**VISUAL SIGNALMAN 2nd CLASS, CPO AND PO**
Open to: 1, 2

**VISUAL SIGNALMAN 2nd CLASS, OTHER RATINGS**
Open to: 3, 4

**VISUAL SIGNALMAN, 3rd CLASS**
Open to: 3, 4

**TRAINED OPERATOR (VISUAL SIGNALS)**
Open to: 4

**SIGNALMAN, NOT TRAINED OPERATOR (VISUAL SIGNALS); ORDINARY SIGNALMAN; SIGNAL BOY; LEADING SIGNALMAN, CONVOY; SIGNALMAN, CONVOY.**
Open to: 3, 4, 5, 6

**SIGNALMAN, LANDING CRAFT**
Open to: 2, 3, 4

**PO CODER; LEADING CODER; ORDINARY CODER; CODER**
Open to: 2, 3. 4, 5

**PO, SHORE SIGNAL SERVICE**
Open to: 2

**SIGNALMAN, SHORE SIGNAL SERVICE**
Open to: 4

**VISUAL SIGNALMAN, BOOM DEFENSE**
Open to: 4

**CHIEF RIGGER, BOOM DEFENSE; RIGGER, BOOM DEFENSE**
Open to: 1, 2

**RIGGER'S MATE, BOOM DEFENSE**
Open to: 3

**DIVER**
Worn by CPO in usual position; by PO and Seaman on right cuff.
Open to: 1, 2, 3, 4

**CHIEF SAILMAKER; SAILMAKER**
Open to: 1, 2

**SAILMAKER'S MATE; FABRIC WORKER**
Open to: 3, 4

**PLATE 21**

**SPECIALTY INSIGNIA; PETTY OFFICERS AND SEAMEN**

LEGEND: 1 = CPO; 2 = PO; 3 = Leading Seaman or equivalent; 4 = Able
Seaman or equivalent; 5 = Ordinary Seaman or equivalent; 6 = Boy.

**BRITISH NAVY**

| | | | | | | | |
|---|---|---|---|---|---|---|---|
|  |  |  |  |  |  |  |  |
| GUNNER'S MATE<br>Open to: 1, 2, 3 | DIRECTOR LAYER, 1st CLASS;<br>GUNLAYER, 1st CLASS<br>Open to: 1, 2, 3 | QUARTERS RATING, 1st CLASS<br>Open to: 1, 2, 3 | QUARTERS RATING, 2nd CLASS<br>Open to: 1, 2, 3, 4 | QUARTERS RATING, 3rd CLASS<br>Open to: 3, 4 | LAYER RATING, 1st CLASS<br>Open to: 1, 2, 3 | LAYER RATING, 2nd CLASS<br>Open to: 1, 2, 3, 4 | LAYER RATING, 3rd CLASS<br>Open to: 3, 4 |
|  |  |  |  |  |  |  |  |
| CONTROL RATING, 1st CLASS<br>Open to: 1, 2, 3 | CONTROL RATING, 2nd CLASS<br>Open to: 1, 2, 3, 4 | CONTROL RATING, 3rd CLASS<br>Open to 3, 4 | ANTI-AIRCRAFT RATING,<br>1st CLASS<br>Open to: 1, 2, 3 | ANTI-A'RCRAFT RATING,<br>2nd CLASS<br>Open to: 1, 2, 3, 4 | ANTI-AIRCRAFT RATING,<br>3rd CLASS<br>Open to: 3, 4 | CPO AND PO GUNNER<br>Open to: 1, 2 | GUNNERY INSTRUCTOR,<br>PATROL SERVICE<br>Open to: 1, 2, 3 |
|  |  |  |  |  |  |  |  |
| GUNLAYER, PATROL SERVICE<br>Open to: 2, 3, 4 | SEAMAN GUNNER,<br>PATROL SERVICE<br>Open to: 3, 4 | GUNLAYER, DEFENSIVELY<br>EQUIPPED MERCHANT SHIPS<br>Open to: 2, 3, 4 | SEAMAN GUNNER,<br>DEFENSIVELY EQUIPPED<br>MERCHANT SHIPS<br>Open to: 3, 4 | SMALL VESSEL GUNLAYER,<br>BOOM DEFENSE<br>Open to: 4, 5 | QUARTERS RATING 3rd CLASS,<br>BOOM DEFENSE<br>Open to: 3, 4 | RANGETAKER, 1st CLASS<br>Open to: 1, 2, 3 | SURVEYING RECORDER<br>Open to: 1, 2, 3, 4 |
|  |  |  |  |  |  |  |  |
| WIRELESS TELEGRAPHIST,<br>1st CLASS<br>Open to: 1, 2, 3 | WIRELESS TELEGRAPHIST<br>2nd CLASS, CPO AND PO<br>Open to: 1, 2 | WIRELESS TELEGRAPHIST,<br>2nd CLASS, OTHER RATINGS<br>Open to: 3, 4 | WIRELESS TELEGRAPHIST,<br>3rd CLASS<br>Open to: 3, 4 | TRAINED OPERATOR<br>(WIRELESS TELEGRAPHIST)<br>Open to: 4 | TELEGRAPHIST, NOT TRAIN-<br>ED OPERATOR (WIRELESS TEL-<br>EGRAPHIST); ORDINARY TEL-<br>EGRAPHIST; BOY TELEGRA-<br>PHIST; RADAR OPERATOR;<br>LEADING TELEGRAPHIST (SPE-<br>CIAL OPERATOR); TELEGRA-<br>PHIST (Sp. Op.); ORDINARY<br>TELEGRAPHIST (Sp. Op.)<br>Open to: 2, 3, 4, 5, 6 | PO, SHORE WIRELESS SERVICE<br>Open to: 2 | TELEGRAPHIST, SHORE<br>WIRELESS SERVICE<br>Open to: 4 |

PLATE 22

**SPECIALTY INSIGNIA; PETTY OFFICERS AND SEAMEN**

LEGEND: 1 = CPO; 2 = PO; 3 = Leading Seaman or equivalent; 4 = Able Seaman or equivalent; 5 = Ordinary Seaman or equivalent; 6 = Boy.

**BRITISH NAVY**

| | | | |
|---|---|---|---|
| SUBMARINE DETECTOR INSTRUCTOR Open to 1, 2, 3 | HIGHER SUBMARINE DETECTOR Open to: 1, 2, 3, 4 | SUBMARINE DETECTOR Open to: 3, 4 | HARBOUR DEFENSE OPERATOR, 1st CLASS. Open to: 2 |

| | | | |
|---|---|---|---|
| HARBOUR DEFENSE OPERATOR, 2nd CLASS Open to: 3 | HARBOUR DEFENSE OPERATOR, 3rd CLASS Open to: 4 | TORPEDO GUNNER'S MATE Open to: 1, 2, 3 | TORPEDO COXSWAIN; COASTAL FORCE COXSWAIN Open to: 1, 2 |

| | | | |
|---|---|---|---|
| LEADING TORPEDOMAN (LOW POWER) Open to: 1, 2, 3, 4 | LEADING TORPEDOMAN Open to: 1, 2, 3, 4 | SEAMAN TORPEDOMAN Open to: 1, 2, 3, 4 | PO WIREMAN Open to: 2 |

| | | | |
|---|---|---|---|
| LEADING WIREMAN Open to: 3 | WIREMAN Open to: 4 | WIREMAN, JOINTER Open to: 2, 3, 4 | PO, CONTROLLED MINING Open to: 2 |

| | | | |
|---|---|---|---|
| LEADING WIREMAN, CONTROLLED MINING Open to: 3 | WIREMAN, CONTROLLED MINING Open to: 4 | LEADING WATCHKEEPER, CONTROLLED MINING; WATCHKEEPER, CONTROLLED MINING Open to: 3, 4 | PO, CONTROLLED MINING STATIONS Open to: 2 |

| | | | |
|---|---|---|---|
| LEADING WIREMAN, CONTROLLED MINING STATIONS Open to: 3 | WIREMAN, CONTROLLED MINING STATIONS Open to: 4 | PO WIREMAN, LANDING CRAFT Open to: 2 | LEADING WIREMAN, LANDING CRAFT Open to: 3 |

| | | | |
|---|---|---|---|
| WIREMAN, LANDING CRAFT Open to: 4 | PO WIREMAN, MINE SWEEPER Open to: 2 | LEADING WIREMAN, MINE SWEEPER Open to: 3 | WIREMAN, MINE SWEEPER Open to: 4 |

| | | | |
|---|---|---|---|
| TORPEDO RATING, BOOM DEFENSE Open to: 3, 4 | CPO AND PO PHOTOGRAPHER Open to: 1, 2 | LEADING PHOTOGRAPHER Open to: 3 | PHOTOGRAPHER Open to: 4 |

J.A.N.NO.1: AUGUST 1944 DIVISION OF NAVAL INTELLIGENCE

**PLATE 23**

**SPECIALTY INSIGNIA; PETTY OFFICERS AND SEAMEN**

LEGEND: 1 = CPO; 2 = PO; 3 = Leading Seaman or equivalent; 4 = Able
Seaman or equivalent; 5 = Ordinary Seaman or equivalent; 6 = Boy.

**BRITISH NAVY**

**RATING OBSERVER**
Open to: 1, 2

**ACTING RATING OBSERVER**
Open to: 2

**TELEGRAPHIST AIR GUNNER, 1st CLASS**
Open to: 1, 2

**TELEGRAPHIST AIR GUNNER, 2nd CLASS**
Open to: 1, 2, 3

**TELEGRAPHIST AIR GUNNER, 3rd CLASS**
Open to: 1, 2, 3, 4

**AIR MECHANIC, AIR FRAME, CPO AND PO**
Open to: 1, 2

**AIR MECHANIC, AIR FRAME, LEADING RATING**
Open to: 3, 4

**AIR MECHANIC, AIR FRAME, OTHER RATINGS**
Open to: 4, 5

**AIR MECHANIC, ENGINE, CPO AND PO**
Open to: 1, 2

**AIR MECHANIC, ENGINE, LEADING RATING**
Open to: 3, 4

**AIR MECHANIC, ENGINE, OTHER RATINGS**
Open to: 4, 5

**AIR MECHANIC, ELECTRICAL, CPO AND PO**
Open to: 1, 2

**AIR MECHANIC, ELECTRICAL, LEADING RATING**
Open to: 3, 4

**AIR MECHANIC, ELECTRICAL, OTHER RATINGS**
Open to: 4, 5

**AIR MECHANIC, ORDNANCE, CPO AND PO**
Open to: 1, 2

**AIR MECHANIC, ORDNANCE, LEADING RATING**
Open to: 3, 4

**AIR MECHANIC, ORDNANCE, OTHER RATINGS**
Open to: 4, 5

**AIR MECHANIC, UNCLASSIFIED**
Open to: 5

**AIR FITTER, AIR FRAME, CPO, PO, LEADING RATING**
Open to: 1, 2, 3

**AIR FITTER, AIR FRAME, OTHER RATINGS**
Open to: 4

**AIR FITTER, ENGINE, CPO, PO, LEADING RATING**
Open to: 1, 2, 3

**AIR FITTER, ENGINE, OTHER RATINGS**
Open to: 4

**AIR FITTER, ELECTRICAL, CPO, PO, LEADING RATING**
Open to: 1, 2, 3

**AIR FITTER, ELECTRICAL, OTHER RATINGS**
Open to: 4

**AIR FITTER, ORDNANCE, CPO, PO, LEADING RATING**
Open to: 1, 2, 3

**AIR FITTER, ORDNANCE, OTHER RATINGS**
Open to: 4

**AIR FITTER, UNCLASSIFIED**
Open to: 4, 5
(Insignia for AIR FITTER, METAL WORKER, is same as other Air Fitter specialists but with the letters M. W. below propeller).

**PLOTTER; BOMB RANGE MARKER**
For WRENS only

**PHYSICAL AND RECREATIONAL TRAINING INSTRUCTOR, 1st CLASS**
Open to: 1, 2, 3, 4

**PHYSICAL AND RECREATIONAL TRAINING INSTRUCTOR, 2nd CLASS**
Open to: 1, 2, 3, 4

**MASTER-AT-ARMS**
Open to: 1

**REGULATING PO**
Open to: 2

PLATE 24

## SPECIALTY INSIGNIA; PETTY OFFICERS AND SEAMEN

LEGEND: 1 = CPO; 2 = PO; 3 = Leading Seaman or equivalent; 4 = Able Seaman or equivalent; 5 = Ordinary Seaman or equivalent; 6 = Boy.

**BRITISH NAVY**

**CHIEF SHIPWRIGHT**
Open to: 1

**CHIEF:—JOINER, BLACKSMITH, PLUMBER, PAINTER, COOPER; also 1st, 2nd, 3rd, 4th (CONFIRMED) CLASS:—SHIPWRIGHT, JOINER, BLACKSMITH, PLUMBER, PAINTER, COOPER**
Open to: 1, 2

**ARTISAN, 4th (ACTING) AND 5th CLASS**
Open to: 2, 3

**MECHANICIAN**
Open to: 1, 2

**CPO AND PO STOKER**
Open to: 1, 2

**LEADING STOKER; STOKER, 1st CLASS**
Open to: 3, 4

**STOKER, 2nd CLASS**
Open to: 5

**STOKER, FIRE FIGHTER**
Open to: to 5
(Higher ratings have letters F.F. below other Stoker insignia)

**CHIEF MOTOR MECHANIC**
Open to: 1 (PO Motor Mechanic has propellor with crown above and star below.)

**MOTOR MECHANIC**
Open to: 3

**WRITER**
Open to: 1, 2, 3, 4, 5

**SUPPLY RATING**
Open to: 1, 2, 3, 4, 5

**COOK**
Open to: 1, 2, 3, 4, 5

**OFFICER'S STEWARD**
Open to: 1, 2, 3, 4, 5

**OFFICER'S COOK**
Open to: 1, 2, 3, 4, 5

**GENERAL DUTIES**
For WRENS only

**MOTOR DRIVER; DESPATCH RIDER**
For WRENS only

**SICK BERTH RATING**

**DENTAL SURGERY ATTENDANT**
Open to: 1, 2, 3, 4, 5

**DENTAL MECHANIC**
Open to: 1, 2, 3, 4, 5

**LABORATORY ASSISTANT**
Open to: 1, 2, 3, 4, 5

**MASSEUR**
Open to: 1, 2, 3, 4, 5

**OPERATING ROOM ASSISTANT**
Open to: 1, 2, 3, 4, 5

**X-RAY ASSISTANT**
Open to: 1, 2, 3, 4, 5

## SPECIAL SERVICE INSIGNIA

J.A.N. NO.1:
AUGUST 1944
DIVISION OF
NAVAL
INTELLIGENCE

**PILOT INSIGNIA**
Worn on right cuff by CPO; on right upper arm by PO.

**FLYING INSIGNIA, RATING OBSERVER AND ACTING RATING OBSERVER**
Worn on left cuff.

**FLYING INSIGNIA, TELEGRAPHIST AIR GUNNERS 1st, 2nd, 3rd AND ACTING 3rd CLASS**
Worn on left cuff.

**COMBINED OPERATIONS, ALL RATINGS**
Navy uniform—on right cuff; Army-type battle dress—on both shoulders.

**COMBINED OPERATIONS COXSWAIN**

**BUGLER**
Worn only by Boys and Seamen without specialty. Right cuff.

**GOOD SHOOTING BADGE**
Worn on right cuff.

**BOMB DISPOSAL BADGE**
Worn on right cuff.

# PLATE 25

**COMMISSIONED OFFICERS**

**FRENCH NAVY**

**CAPTAIN**
Capitaine de Vaisseau

SEA CAP FOR VICE ADMIRAL

SEA CAP INSIGNIA FOR VICE ADMIRAL
Two stars for Rear Admiral

CAP BRAID FOR VICE ADMIRAL
Replaces plain band on Sea Cap.
Worn with Cap Insignia below.

CAP BRAID FOR REAR ADMIRAL

**CAP INSIGNIA FOR FLAG OFFICERS**
Worn with Cap Braid above

**LIEUTENANT**
Lieutenant de Vaisseau

CAP FOR ENSIGN
Rank for other Officers below Flag Rank is
indicated by same stripes as on sleeve, except for Midshipmen

CAP INSIGNIA FOR OFFICERS
BELOW FLAG RANK
Silver for Administrators and Civil Engineers

CAP INSIGNIA FOR MIDSHIPMEN
Worn with single stripe on cap band

**STEEL HELMET**
Worn at sea

**ENSIGN**
Enseigne de Vaisseau, 2me Classe
(Identical khaki uniform optional)

I.A.N. No. 1: JULY 1943.

PLATE 26

## SHOULDER BOARDS AND SLEEVE INSIGNIA: LINE OFFICERS

FRENCH NAVY

  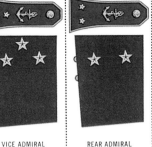       

| VICE ADMIRAL (In Command of Forces) Vice-Amiral (Commandement en chef) | VICE ADMIRAL Vice-Amiral | REAR ADMIRAL Contre-Amiral | CAPTAIN Capitaine de Vaisseau | COMMANDER Capitaine de Frégate | LIEUTENANT COMMANDER Capitaine de Corvette | LIEUTENANT Lieutenant de Vaisseau | LIEUTENANT (jg) Enseigne de Vaisseau de 1re Classe | ENSIGN Enseigne de Vaisseau de 2me Classe | MIDSHIPMAN Aspirant |

## SHOULDER BOARDS AND SLEEVE INSIGNIA: COMMISSIONED ENLISTED CORPS   OTHER CORPS

The Commissioned Enlisted Corps, having no Corps color, is distinguished by the vertical patch on top of the stripes. There is no anchor on the shoulder board. Commissioned from the ranks, these Officers can hold rank from Lieutenant (jg) to Commander. For titles and method of address see text on back of separator sheet.

| LIEUTENANT (jg), COMMISSIONED ENLISTED CORPS Officier de 2me Classe, Equipages de la Flotte | LIEUTENANT (jg), COMMISSIONED ENLISTED CORPS Officier de 2me Classe, Equipages de la Flotte | CAPTAIN, DOCTOR Médecin en Chef de 1re Classe | COMMANDER, DOCTOR Médecin en Chef de 2me Classe | LIEUTENANT COMMANDER, MECHANICAL ENGINEER Ingénieur-Mécanicien Principal | LIEUTENANT MECHANICAL ENGINEER Ingénieur-Mécanicien de 1re Classe | LIEUTENANT (jg), SUPPLY Commissaire de 2me Classe | ENSIGN, SUPPLY Commissaire de 3me Classe |

## SPECIALTY INSIGNIA—AVIATION

SPECIAL INSIGNIA — Worn on breast

All properly qualified personnel, regardless of rank, are entitled to wear the five adjoining insignia.

The insignia at the immediate right is worn by the following:
AVIATION OBSERVERS Observateurs d'Aviation
AVIATION MECHANICS—Mécaniciens Volants
AVIATION RADIOMEN—Radiotélégraphistes Volants
MACHINE GUNNERS AND BOMBARDIERS - Mitrailleurs-Bombardiers

| Worn on right breast by personnel as indicated in the text at the immediate left. | PILOTS Pilotes d'Aviation (Worn on right breast) | CAPTIVE BALLOON OBSERVERS Observateurs en Ballon Captif (Worn on right breast) | DIRIGIBLE PILOTS Pilotes de Dirigeable (Worn on right breast) | AIR PERSONNEL Personnel de l'Aéronautique (Worn on upper left sleeve) | CROSS OF LORRAINE Croix de Lorraine (Worn by "Fighting French") | ATHLETIC INSTRUCTORS Instructeurs d'Exercices Physiques |

## SHOULDER INSIGNIA — Worn on blue uniform

BUTTONS

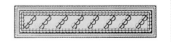     

| FLAG OFFICERS | SENIOR OFFICERS Captain to Lieutenant Commander | JUNIOR OFFICERS Lieutenant to Ensign | MIDSHIPMEN | FLAG OFFICERS | OFFICERS BELOW FLAG RANK |

J.A.N. No. 1: JULY 1943.

PLATE 27

**PETTY OFFICERS**

**CAP FOR PETTY OFFICERS**
Chief P.O. and P.O. 1st Class
wear one stripe on cap band

CAP INSIGNIA

STEEL HELMET
Worn at sea

SENIOR CHIEF PETTY OFFICER
Maître Principal

PETTY OFFICER, 1st CLASS
Maître
(Old style uniform)

PETTY OFFICER, 2nd CLASS
Second-Maître, 1re Classe

PETTY OFFICER, 3rd CLASS
Second-Maître, 2me Classe
(Identical khaki uniform optional)

J.A.N. No. 1: JULY 1943.

PLATE 28

## SLEEVE INSIGNIA: PETTY OFFICERS

SPECIALTY SLEEVE INSIGNIA

FRENCH NAVY

**SENIOR CHIEF PETTY OFFICER**
Maître Principal

**CHIEF PETTY OFFICER**
Premier Maître

**PETTY OFFICER, 1st CLASS**
Maître

**PETTY OFFICER, 2nd CLASS**
Second-Maître, 1re Classe

**PETTY OFFICER, 3rd CLASS**
Second-Maître, 2me Classe

These insignia are worn on the sleeves (around the edge of the cuff and on the upper arms, respectively) in addition to the usual insignia of rank.

**BUGLER**
Clairon

**YEOMAN**
Fourrier

BUTTON

**PETTY OFFICERS**

## SHOULDER BOARDS — Worn on white and khaki uniforms

SHOULDER INSIGNIA

**SENIOR CHIEF PETTY OFFICER**
Maître Principal

**CHIEF PETTY OFFICER**
Premier Maître

**PETTY OFFICER, 1st CLASS**
Maître

**PETTY OFFICER, 2nd CLASS**
Second-Maître, 1re Classe

**PETTY OFFICER, 3rd CLASS**
Second-Maître, 2me Classe

**CHIEF PETTY OFFICERS**
Worn on blue uniform

## SPECIALTY INSIGNIA — Worn on upper left sleeve

**AVIATION PERSONNEL**
Personnel Spécialiste et Navigant de l'Aéronautique

**AVIATION RADIOMAN**
Radiotélégraphiste de l'Aéronautique

**SUBMARINE CREW**
Equipage de Sous-marin

**FENCING MASTER**
Maître d'Armes

**ATHLETIC INSTRUCTOR**
Instructeur d'Exercices Physiques
(Worn on left breast)

**RANGE FINDER OPERATOR**
Télémétriste

**GUNNER**
Fusilier

**MASTER GUN LAYER**
Télépointeur Superieur

**GUN LAYER**
Télépointeur Élémentaire

**STAR FOR HIGHEST PROFICIENCY**
Worn just above Range Finder, Gunner, and Gun Layer Insignia

**STAR FOR HIGH PROFICIENCY**
Worn just above Range Finder, Gunner, and Gun Layer Insignia

**STAR FOR PROFICIENCY**
Worn just above Range Finder, Gunner, and Gun Layer Insignia

## COLLAR INSIGNIA — Worn on both sides of collar

J.A.N. No. 1:
JULY 1943.

**FLEET PILOT**
Pilote de la Flotte

**MILITARY INSPECTOR**
Surveillant Militaire

**AUXILIARY GUARD**
Garde Consigne Auxiliaire

**SHORE SIGNALMAN**
Guetteur Sémaphorique

**FIREMAN**
Pompier

**HARBOR PILOT**
Direction de Port

**MUSICIAN**
Musicien

**SUPERIOR CERTIFICATE**
Breveté Supérieur

**AVIATION PILOT SECTION CHIEF**
Pilote Chef de Section

# PLATE 29

**SEAMEN**

**FRENCH NAVY**

SEAMAN, 1st CLASS
Quartier-Maître 1re Classe

SEAMAN, 1st CLASS
Quartier-Maître 1re Classe
(Tropical uniform)

DEBARKATION HELMET

TROPICAL UNIFORM INSIGNIA
Seaman, 1st Class—three stripes
Seaman, 2nd Class—two stripes
Seaman, 3rd Class—one stripe

WORKING CAP
Chauffeurs and Machinists

CAP INSIGNIA

STEEL HELMET
Worn at sea

SEAMAN, 2nd CLASS
Quartier-Maître 2me Classe
(Debarkation uniform)

SEAMAN, 3rd CLASS
ELEMENTARY CERTIFICATE,
YEOMAN
Matelot Breveté Élémentaire, Fourrier

J.A.N. No. 1: JULY 1943.

PLATE 30

## SLEEVE INSIGNIA: SEAMEN

The insignia at the immediate right is worn by the graduates of Petty Officer School. These Seamen usually have not served in the elementary ranks and are shortly to be promoted to Petty Officer.

**SEAMAN, GRADUATE OF PETTY OFFICER SCHOOL**
Quartier-Maître, École de Maistrance

**SEAMAN, 1st CLASS**
Quartier-Maître 1re Classe

**SEAMAN, 2nd CLASS**
Quartier-Maître 2me Classe

**SEAMAN, 3rd CLASS, ELEMENTARY CERTIFICATE**
Matelot Breveté Élémentaire

**SEAMAN, 3rd CLASS, PROVISIONAL CERTIFICATE**
Matelot Breveté Provisoire
(Upper left sleeve only)

## SPECIALTY INSIGNIA

The two insignia at the immediate right (worn along the edge of the cuff and on the upper arms, respectively) are worn in addition to the usual insignia of rank

**BUGLER**
Clairon

## FRENCH NAVY

**YEOMAN**
Fourrier

## SPECIALTY INSIGNIA — Worn on upper left sleeve

These insignia, when worn by Seamen 3rd Class with an Elementary Certificate, indicate that the wearer usually has had training in a similar or allied field in civilian life, unlike the Seamen 3rd Class with a Provisional Certificate who lack this training.

**AVIATION PERSONNEL**
Personnel Spécialiste et Naviguant de l'Aéronautique

**AVIATION RADIOMAN**
Radiotélégraphiste de l'Aéronautique

**SUPERIOR CERTIFICATE**
Breveté Supérieur
(Worn just above rank stripes)

**ALL NON-P O PERSONNEL**
Equipages de la Flotte
(Upper right sleeve of blue uniform)

**ANTI-AIRCRAFT MACHINE GUNNER**
Fusilier-Mitrailleur Contre Avions
(Gold indicates proficiency)

**ANTI-AIRCRAFT MACHINE GUNNER**
Fusilier-Mitrailleur Contre Avions

**MACHINE GUNNER OR MASTER GUNNER**
Fusilier-Mitrailleur; Quartier-Maître Breveté Supérieur Fusilier

**GUNNER**
Fusilier

**RADIOMAN, GENERAL SERVICE**
Radiotélégraphiste, Service Général

**RADIOMAN, COASTAL SERVICE**
Radiocôtier

**CHAUFFEUR**
Conducteur d'Automobile

**SUBMARINE CREW**
Equipage de Sous-marin

**FENCING MASTER**
Maître d'Armes

**FENCING INSTRUCTOR**
Prévôt d'Armes

**RECRUITED MUSICIAN**
Musicien de Recrutement

**AUXILIARY FIREMAN**
Pompier Auxiliaire

**SHORE COMMUNICATIONS**
Transmissions Sédentaires

**RANGE FINDER OPERATOR**
Télémétriste

**GUN AIMER**
Pointeur d'Artillerie

**MASTER GUN LAYER**
Télépointeur Supérieur

**GUN LAYER**
Télépointeur Élémentaire

**STAR FOR HIGHEST PROFICIENCY**
Worn just above Range Finder, Gun Aimer, and Gun Layer insignia

**STAR FOR HIGH PROFICIENCY**
Worn just above Range Finder, Gun Aimer, and Gun Layer insignia

**STAR FOR PROFICIENCY**
Worn just above Range Finder, Gun Aimer, and Gun Layer insignia

**ARMBAND FOR HOSPITAL CORPSMAN**
Brassard d'Infirmier

## SPECIALTY INSIGNIA — Worn on collar

These insignia, unless otherwise indicated, are to be worn on both sides of the collar of the Petty Officer type uniform. Shore Signalmen, Shore Firemen, Harbor Pilots, and Musicians wear the Petty Officer uniform instead of the jumper-type Seaman uniform.

J A N. No. 1: JULY 1943.

**SHORE SIGNALMAN**
Guetteur Sémaphorique

**SHORE FIREMAN**
Pompier

**HARBOR PILOT**
Direction de Port

**MUSICIAN**
Musicien

**ALL NON-P.O. PERSONNEL**
Equipages de la Flotte
(Both sides of overcoat collar)

## SPECIALTY INSIGNIA — Worn on breast

The two insignia illustrated at the immediate right are worn on the left breast. The use of these insignia is optional.

**ATHLETIC INSTRUCTOR**
Instructeur d'Exercices Physiques

**INTERPRETER**
Interprète

## PLATE 31

**COMMISSIONED, WARRANT AND 1st CLASS PETTY OFFICERS**

**LIEUTENANT (jg) (Line)**
Oberleutnant zur See

**CAPTAIN'S CAP**

**SHOULDER INSIGNIA**

**SENIOR MIDSHIPMAN (MEDICAL)**
Oberfähnrich (Sanitäts)
Ranks with Warrant Officer

**MIDSHIPMAN**
Fähnrich
Ranks with Petty Officer, 2nd Class

**SLEEVE INSIGNIA**

**PROBATIONARY MIDSHIPMAN**
Seekadett
Ranks with Seaman, 2nd Class. Cadets and
Midshipmen wear on left sleeve the insignia of
their future Officer Corps.

**OVERSEAS CAP FOR ALL PERSONNEL**
Gold piping denotes officer rank

**NATIONAL EMBLEM**

**BUTTON**

**SHOULDER DEVICE**
Used to denote rank

**CAP DEVICE FOR ALL OFFICERS IN GERMAN NAVY**

**CAP, WARRANT, CHIEF AND
1st CLASS PETTY OFFICERS**

**SHOULDER INSIGNIA**
WARRANT, CHIEF and
1st CLASS PETTY OFFICERS

**CHIEF SHIP'S CLERK**
Schreiberstabsoberfeldwebel

**MACHINIST**
Obermaschinist

**CHIEF QUARTERMASTER**
Stabssteuermann

**BOATSWAIN'S MATE, 1st CLASS**
Bootsmann

**BOATSWAIN'S MATE, 1st CLASS**
Bootsmann

J.A.N. No. 1: FEBRUARY 1943

**PLATE 32**

## SHOULDER AND SLEEVE INSIGNIA;
COMMISSIONED OFFICERS

**GERMAN NAVY**

|  |  |  | |  |  |  |  |  |  |
|---|---|---|---|---|---|---|---|---|---|
|  |  |  |  |  |  |  |  | |  |
| **ADMIRAL** Admiral Line | **VICE ADMIRAL** Vizeadmiral Medical | **REAR ADMIRAL** Konteradmiral Engineering | **COMMODORE** Kommodore Ordnance | **CAPTAIN** Kapitän zur See Technical Communications | **COMMANDER** Fregattenkapitän Administration | **LIEUTENANT COMMANDER** Korvettenkapitän Defensive Ordnance | **LIEUTENANT** Kapitänleutnant Naval Coast Artillery | **LIEUTENANT. (jg)** Oberleutnant zur See Communications Reserve | **ENSIGN** Leutnant zur See Line |

**CORP INSIGNIA**—Worn on Sleeves and Shoulder Marks. Two oak leaves beneath the insignia denote reserve officers. **LINE INSIGNIA** is worn on sleeves only.

| | | | | | | | | |
|---|---|---|---|---|---|---|---|---|
| **LINE** Seeoffizier | **MEDICAL** Sanitätsoffizier | **ENGINEERING** Ingenieuroffizier | **ORDNANCE** Waffenoffizier | **TECHNICAL COMMUNICATIONS** Technische Nachrichtenwesen | **ADMINISTRATION** Verwaltungsoffizier | **DEFENSIVE ORDNANCE** Waffenoffizier (Sperrwaffen) | **NAVAL COAST ARTILLERY** Marineartillerie | **COMMUNICATIONS RESERVE** Marinenachrichtenoffizier des Beurlaubtenstandes |

**INSIGNIA** — CIVILIAN NAVAL OFFICIALS — MARINEBEAMTEN

Officials wear uniforms like the equivalent rank of Commissioned, Warrant, or Petty Officers except that the buttons, braid, national emblems and rank badges are silver. Officials equivalent to Commissioned Officers wear silver cords on caps. Officials' corps insignia are worn on sleeve above rank stripes, or on shoulder marks, which have colored piping in various colors: administrative, pharmacist, and non-technical instructors, cornflower blue; legal officials, carmine red; technical officials, pilots, and technical instructors, black.

|  |  |  |  |  |  |  |
|---|---|---|---|---|---|---|
| **INSTRUCTOR** Lehrer Higher commissioned | **PHARMACIST** Marineapotheker Higher commissioned | **DENTIST** Marinezahnarzt | **LEGAL OFFICER** Justizbeamte Lower commissioned | **TECHNICIANS** Technische Beamte Lower commissioned | **ENGINE-ROOM TECHNICIAN** Seemaschinisten Lower commissioned | **ADMINISTRATIVE** Verwaltungsbeamte Non-commissioned |

J.A.N. No. 1. FEBRUARY 1943

PLATE 33

**PETTY OFFICERS, 2nd AND 3rd CLASS, AND SEAMEN**

CAP

OVERSEAS CAP
Worn at sea

STEEL HELMET

EAGLE OF ARMED FORCES
Worn on left side of helmet

NATIONAL COLORS
Worn on right side of helmet

**MACHINIST'S MATE, 2nd CLASS**
Obermaschinenmaat
Service dress

**MACHINIST'S MATE, 3rd CLASS**
Maschinenmaat
Summer uniform

**SEAMAN, 1st CLASS**
Matrosenobergefreiter
Summer uniform

**SEAMAN, 2nd CLASS**
Signalgefreiter
Landing rig

J.A.N. No. 1: FEBRUARY 1943

**PLATE 34**

# PETTY OFFICERS, 2ND AND 3RD CLASS AND SEAMEN

**GERMAN NAVY**

## RATING INSIGNIA
Upper left sleeve

MACHINIST'S MATE, 2nd CLASS
Obermaschinenmaat

STOREKEEPER, 3rd CLASS
Verwaltungsmaat

COXSWAIN (Boatswain's Mate, 3rd class)
Bootsmannsmaat

QUARTERMASTER, 3rd CLASS
Steuermannsmaat

NATIONAL EMBLEM

BUTTON

ADMIRAL'S FLAG
Worn by personnel of Admiral's staff,
on left sleeve above insignia

## RATING INSIGNIA
Upper left sleeve

SEAMAN, 1st CLASS
(HIGHEST RATED)
Matrosenhauptgefreiter

SEAMAN, 1st CLASS
Matrosenhauptgefreiter

SEAMAN, 2nd CLASS
(Awaiting promotion to Petty Officer)
Matrosengefreiter (Unteroffizieranwärter)

SEAMAN, 2nd CLASS
Matrosengefreiter

## SERVICE BADGES—Indicating action in this war **in the type of service portrayed—Worn on left breast below pocket.**

SUBMARINE, 1939 | DESTROYER | MINESWEEPER AND SUBMARINE CHASER | NAVAL ARTILLERY | AUXILIARY CRUISER | BATTLESHIP AND CRUISER | BLOCKADE RUNNER | TORPEDO BOAT

## CORPS INSIGNIA—Worn on upper left sleeve above rating insignia—Superimposed on anchor in the case of Petty Officers.

BOATSWAIN (SEAMAN)
Bootsmanns-Laufbahn (Matrose) | SIGNALMAN
Signal- | TELEGRAPHER
Fernschreib- | CARPENTER
Zimmermann- | ORDNANCE ENGINEER
Artillerie-Mechaniker- | TORPEDO ENGINEER
Torpedo-Mechaniker- | MINE ENGINEER
Sperr-Mechaniker- | STOREKEEPER
Verwaltung

YEOMAN
Schreiber- | PHARMACIST
Sanität- | MUSICIAN
Musik | MACHINIST
Maschinen | RADIOMAN
Funk- | NAVAL ARTILLERYMAN
Marine-Artillerie | MOTOR TRANSPORT ASHORE
Kraftfahr- | AIRCRAFT SPOTTER
Flugmelde-

J.A.N. No.1
1 FEBRUARY 1943

PLATE 35

**FIELD GRAY UNIFORM: OFFICERS AND MEN** — OF NAVAL ARTILLERY

**LIEUTENANT (jg)**
Oberleutnant zur See

**OFFICER'S CAP**
Silver cord indicates commissioned rank.

**CAP DEVICE**
Worn by all officers in German Navy

**BUTTON**

**SHOULDER DEVICE**
Used to denote rank

**CHIEF PETTY OFFICER**
Stabsfeldwebel

**OVERSEAS CAP**
For Petty Officers 2nd class and below

**NATIONAL EMBLEM**

**BELT BUCKLE**
Worn with black leather belts by Warrant and Petty Officers. Commissioned officers wear brown leather belts with plain buckle.

**COLLAR PATCH**

**SEAMAN, 2nd CLASS**
Gefreiter

PLATE 36

# FIELD GRAY UNIFORM—SHOULDER INSIGNIA—COMMISSIONED OFFICERS

J A N No 1  FEBRUARY 1943

## GERMAN NAVY

COMMODORE or CAPTAIN
Kommodore oder Kapitän zur See

COMMANDER
Fregattenkapitän

LIEUTENANT COMMANDER
Korvettenkapitän

LIEUTENANT
Kapitänleutnant

LIEUTENANT (jg)
Oberleutnant zur See

ENSIGN
Leutnant zur See

## SHOULDER INSIGNIA — WARRANT, CHIEF, AND PETTY OFFICERS, 1st CLASS

## SHOULDER INSIGNIA — PETTY OFFICERS 2nd AND 3rd CLASS, AND SEAMEN

CHIEF WARRANT OFFICER, SAILORS' POOL, BALTIC
Stabsoberfeldwebel,
Schiffsstammabteilung der Ostsee

WARRANT OFFICER, 4th COAST ARTILLERY
Oberfeldwebel, IV Marineartillerieabteilung

CHIEF PETTY OFFICER, SAILORS' POOL, NORTH SEA
Stabsfeldwebel (F),
Schiffsstammabteilung der Nordsee

PETTY OFFICER, 1st CLASS, 2nd COAST ARTILLERY
Feldwebel, II Marineartillerieabteilung

Field gray uniforms are worn only ashore by Naval Artillery detachments or by trainees at shore establishments. The uniform is the same as the Army's except that the Navy buttons and National Emblem are gold instead of gray, and the Navy shoulder marks carry no piping. Seamen in field gray uniforms wear insignia both on shoulders and on left sleeve; Petty Officers wear insignia only on shoulders. Commissioned Officers wear the same marks as on white uniforms. Warrant Officers wear two gold sleeve stripes. Sonderführer, appointed for special duties during war time, wear an anchor device on both lapels of their blouses. Since field gray uniforms are worn only for certain sorts of activity, not all Corps are represented on the shoulder marks. The letters N (North Sea) and O (Baltic Sea) no longer appear.

PETTY OFFICER, 2nd CLASS, PETTY OFFICERS' SCHOOL
Obermaat, Marine-Unteroffizierlehrabteilung

PETTY OFFICER, 3rd CLASS, 1st DETACHMENT AIRCRAFT SPOTTERS
Maat, Flugmeldeabteilung I

PETTY OFFICER ASPIRANT, SAILORS' POOL, BALTIC
Unteroffizieranwärter,
Schiffsstammabteilung der Ostsee

SEAMAN, SAILORS' POOL, NORTH SEA
Matrose der Schiffsstammabteilung der Nordsee

## RATING INSIGNIA

SEAMEN

Worn on upper left sleeve

SEAMAN, 1st CLASS (Obsolete)
Stabsgefreiter

SEAMAN, 1st CLASS (Old Style)
Obergefreiter

SEAMAN, 1st CLASS (HIGHEST RATED)
Hauptgefreiter

SEAMAN, 1st CLASS
Obergefreiter

SEAMAN, 2nd CLASS
Gefreiter

## CORPS INSIGNIA

COMMISSIONED OFFICERS

Worn by Commissioned Officers on shoulder marks. Line Officers' stars are not worn on field gray uniforms. Two oak leaves beneath the insignia indicate Reserve Officers.

LINE
Seeoffizier

ADMINISTRATIVE
Verwaltungsoffizier

MEDICAL
Sanitätsoffizier

DEFENSIVE ORDNANCE
Waffenoffizier (Sperrwaffen)

ENGINEERING
Ingenieuroffizier

NAVAL COAST ARTILLERY
Offizier des Marineartillerie

ORDNANCE
Waffenoffizier

COMMUNICATIONS
Marinenachrichtenoffizier

TECHNICAL COMMUNICATIONS
Offizier des technischen Nachrichtenwesens

COMMUNICATIONS (RESERVE)
Marinenachrichtenoffizier des Beurlaubtenstandes

PLATE 37

# CIVILIAN NAVAL OFFICIALS

**CORPS INSIGNIA** — Worn below eagle on sleeve or shoulder board.

**ADMINISTRATIVE OFFICIALS**
Verwaltungsbeamten
(Highest Group)

**ADMINISTRATIVE OFFICIALS**
Verwaltungsbeamten
(Advanced Group)

**ADMINISTRATIVE OFFICIALS**
Verwaltungsbeamten
(Intermediate and Lowest Groups)

**LEGAL OFFICIALS**
Justizbeamten
(Highest Group)

**LEGAL OFFICIALS**
Justizbeamten
(Advanced Group)

**LEGAL OFFICIALS**
Justizbeamten
(Intermediate and Lowest Groups)

**TECHNICAL OFFICIALS**
Technische Beamten
(Highest Group)

**SEA SERVICE OFFICIALS**
Seemännischer Fahrzeugbeamten
(Advanced Group)

**SEA SERVICE OFFICIALS**
Seemännischer Fahrzeugbeamten
(Intermediate and Lowest Groups)

Civilian Naval Officials (Marinebeamten) are administrative personnel attached to the Navy. In wartime they wear naval uniforms on which the buttons, sleeve stripes, national emblem, Corps and cap insignia are in silver. They hold rank equivalent to that of regular naval personnel, but with the ranks of Chief Petty Officer and Chief Warrant Officer omitted. The various Corps are divided into groups to indicate restrictions in rank as follows: Lowest, PO 1st Class and Warrant Officer; Intermediate, Warrant Officer through Lieutenant (jg); Advanced, Lieutenant (jg) through Commander; and Highest, Lieutenant through Vice Admiral. Transfers between groups are prohibited.

**TECHNICAL OFFICIALS**
Technische Beamten
(Advanced Group)

**TECHNICAL OFFICIALS**
Technische Beamten
(Intermediate and Lowest Groups)

**ENGINE-ROOM TECHNICIANS**
Seemaschinisten Beamten
(Advanced Group)

**ENGINE-ROOM TECHNICIANS**
Seemaschinisten Beamten
(Intermediate and Lowest Groups)

**SLEEVE STRIPE, COMMISSIONED OFFICERS**
Illustrated here for Lieutenant (jg), Technician

**CORPS INSIGNIA**
Illustrated for Technical Official. Worn above sleeve stripes by Commissioned Officers; on shoulder boards by PO 1st Class and Warrant Officer.

**SHOULDER BOARD**
Illustrated for Warrant Officer, Technician.
PO 1st Class wears only one pip.

**DENTISTS**
Marinezahnärzte
(Highest Group)

**PHARMACISTS**
Marineapotheker
(Highest Group)

**INSTRUCTORS**
Lehrer Beamten
(Highest Group)

**INSTRUCTORS**
Lehrer Beamten
(Advanced Group)

**LABORATORY OFFICIALS**
Werkstattbeamten
(Advanced Group)

**LABORATORY OFFICIALS**
Werkstattbeamten
(Intermediate and Lowest Groups)

## CORPS COLORS; CIVILIAN NAVAL OFFICIALS

**SHOULDER BOARD; LEGAL OFFICIAL**
Illustrated for Lieutenant (jg)

Corps colors are limited to Commissioned Officers and are worn only on the shoulder board, as illustrated at left.

Cornflower Blue
**FOR ADMINISTRATIVE OFFICIALS, PHARMACISTS, AND NON-TECHNICAL INSTRUCTORS**

Carmine Red
**FOR LEGAL OFFICIALS**

Black
**FOR TECHNICAL OFFICIALS AND TECHNICAL INSTRUCTORS**

## TEMPORARY CIVILIAN NAVAL OFFICIALS

Civilian Officials attached to Navy for duration only (Marinebeamten auf Kriegsdauer) are of two classes: with and without military training. The latter wear lapel anchors in addition to their other insignia.

**SHOULDER BOARD; COMMISSIONED OFFICERS**
Illustrated for Ensign, Legal Official

**LAPEL ANCHOR**
Worn on jacket lapels by Temporary Civilian Naval Officials without Military Training.

**CORPS INSIGNIA**
Any Corps Insignia illustrated for regular Civilian Naval Officials may be worn by adding the oval as shown above; worn above sleeve stripes.

**SHOULDER BOARD; WARRANT OFFICER**
Petty Officer 1st Class wears only one pip.

**CIVILIAN NAVAL OFFICIAL, TECHNICIAN**
Illustrated as Lieutenant
Note: Flag Officers wear gold chin cords instead of silver.

J.A.N. No. 1
July, 1944
DIVISION OF NAVAL INTELLIGENCE

PLATE 38

# FIELD GRAY AND MISCELLANEOUS; SUPPLEMENT

GERMAN NAVY

**UNIT INSIGNIA, FIELD GRAY UNIFORM** Worn by Warrant and Petty Officers and Seamen only, on shoulder boards.

MISCELLANEOUS

COAST ARTILLERY UNITS
Marineartillerie Abteilungen

SAILOR'S POOL
Schiffsstammabteilung
(This group constitutes a man-power
reservoir for general naval needs)

AIRCRAFT SPOTTER UNITS
Flugmeldeabteilungen

PO INSTRUCTOR UNITS
Marine-Unteroffizier-Lehrabteilungen

RESERVE OFFICERS
The twin oak leaves formerly
worn by Reserve Officers beneath
their Corps Insignia have been
abolished for the duration, so
that Corps Insignia now appears
the same for Regular or Reserve
Officers.

COMMODORE, LINE
The rank of Commodore is restricted
to Line Officers only. The rank of Rear
Admiral. and above, is limited to Line,
Engineering. and Medical Corps.

**SHOULDER BOARDS, FIELD GRAY UNIFORMS** — Warrant and Petty Officers and Seamen. Numerals indicate groups within the Unit.

CHIEF WARRANT OFFICER, COAST ARTILLERY
Stabsoberfeldwebel, Marineartillerie
(Note: CWO is not considered a
Commissioned Officer in the German Navy)

WARRANT OFFICER, COAST ARTILLERY
Oberfeldwebel, Marineartillerie

CHIEF PETTY OFFICER, COAST ARTILLERY
Stabsfeldwebel, Marineartillerie

PETTY OFFICER 1st CLASS, COAST ARTILLERY
Feldwebel, Marineartillerie

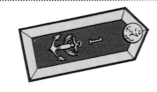

PETTY OFFICER 2nd CLASS, COAST ARTILLERY
Obermaat, Marineartillerie

PETTY OFFICER 3rd CLASS, COAST ARTILLERY
Maat, Marineartillerie

PETTY OFFICER ASPIRANT, COAST ARTILLERY
Unteroffizieranwarter, Marineartillerie
(Worn in conjunction with sleeve chevrons which indi-
cate rank; see J.A.N. No. 1, Revision and Addenda:
July 1944)

ENLISTED MEN BELOW PETTY OFFICER
COAST ARTILLERY
Worn in conjunction with sleeve chevrons which
indicate rank; see J.A.N. No. 1, Revision and
Addenda: July 1944

**COLLAR PATCHES, FIELD GRAY UNIFORM**

MISCELLANEOUS

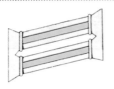

COMMISSIONED OFFICERS

WARRANT AND PETTY OFFICERS
AND SEAMEN

SEAMAN, AWAITING PROMOTION TO PO
Unteroffizieranwarter

SEAMAN, TAKING PO COURSE
Unteroffizierdiensttuer

SPECIALISTS (Sonderführer)
are personnel with particular or
unusual qualifications taken into
the Navy as Commissioned or
Petty Officers without prelimi-
nary training. They are distinguished from regular naval personnel only by the anchor worn
on their lapels. They have fre-
quently acted as plain clothes
agents in foreign countries.

SPECIALISTS'
ANCHOR
Worn on both lapels
by officers and men

WARRANT OFFICER, COAST ARTILLERY
Oberfeldwebel, Marineartillerie.
Note: Differing from all other personnel, commissioned or enlisted, both CWO and WO wear two gold
stripes on sleeves of Field Gray Uniform.

J.A.N. No. 1
July, 1944
DIVISION OF NAVAL INTELLIGENCE

PLATE 39

**REVISION AND ADDENDA**

### OVERSEAS CAP

The axe on the left side is an example of the type of emblem which may be adopted by submarine personnel to represent their particular vessel or flotilla. The chosen emblem is also worn on the left side of the cap with visor.

### SUBMARINE COMMANDER'S CAP

A white cover on the service cap distinguishes a submarine Skipper from the other personnel of the vessel.

### CORPS INSIGNIA

#### COMMISSIONED OFFICERS

Worn above rank stripes on sleeve and shoulder board.

**TORPEDO-TECHNICAL OFFICER**
Torpedo-technischer Offizier

**SHORE DUTY SERVICE**
Allgemeine Marinedienst
This insignia consists of a gold anchor and is worn by personnel restricted to duties on shore.

### WARRANT AND PETTY OFFICERS AND SEAMEN

Warrant Officers, CPO, and PO 1st Class: Superimposed on anchor (see note below for exception) on shoulder board.
PO 2nd and 3rd Class: Superimposed on anchor (with exception noted below) on upper left sleeve.
Seamen: Worn alone on upper left sleeve above Rating Insignia.

**ORDNANCE MAN**
Feuerwerker-

**HYDROGRAPHER**
Vermessungs-

Note: The Quartermaster-Hydrographer Corps (Vermessungssteuer-mannslaufbahn), for Warrant and Petty Officers only, uses as its insignia the Hydrographer's Insignia superimposed on the Quartermaster's crossed anchors.

#### LEATHER SUBMARINE UNIFORM
No insignia is worn. Any regulation cap permissible.

#### OVERCOAT FOR PO 2nd AND 3rd CLASS AND SEAMEN
Illustrated as Boatswain's Mate, 2nd Class.
Higher ratings wear long overcoat.

### OVERCOAT COLLAR PATCHES

Worn by PO 2nd and 3rd Class and Seamen only.
Note: Gold piping around collar (see figure at left) is restricted to Petty Officers.

| PETTY OFFICER, 2nd CLASS | PETTY OFFICER, 3rd CLASS | ALL SEAMEN |

### KHAKI SERVICE UNIFORM

The uniform illustrated at right has been recovered from submarine personnel operating in Atlantic waters. It is identical to Army tropical wear except that the national emblem on blouse and cap is gold rather than silver. The buttons, too, are gold or brown, with the usual naval anchor, rather than the plain silver Army button. The blue overseas cap (illustrated at left above) and long trousers are optional. Officers and men wear the same uniform with the appropriate shoulder or sleeve insignia to indicate rank and specialty.

### SERVICE AND WOUND INSIGNIA

Worn on left breast

**SUBMARINE SERVICE, 1914-1918**

**WOUND INSIGNIA, 1914-1918**     **WOUND INSIGNIA, 1939**

#### KHAKI SERVICE UNIFORM
Illustrated as Boatswain's Mate, 1st Class.
See description at left.

# PLATE 40

## REVISION AND ADDENDA

**SPECIALTY INSIGNIA;** PETTY OFFICERS 2nd AND 3rd CLASS AND SEAMEN.

Specialty Insignia are worn on upper left sleeve below Rating Insignia. The colors are red on blue uniform and overcoat, and cornflower blue on white uniform. These comprise the latest complete set available. It is possible that some of the Specialty Insignia previously illustrated in J.A.N. No. 1 (Feb. 1943) may still be worn.

SUBMARINE RADARMAN
This insignia consists of a small star above three bolts of lightning.

| GUN CAPTAIN (HEAVY ARTILLERY)
Geschützführer (schwere Artillerie) | GUN CAPTAIN (MEDIUM ARTILLERY)
Geschützführer (Mittelartillerie) | GUN CAPTAIN (AA, SMALL VESSEL)
Geschützführer (Flakartillerie, kleines Fahrzeug) | GUN CAPTAIN (HEAVY AA)
Geschützführer (schwere Flakartillerie) | GUN CAPTAIN (LIGHT AA)
Geschützführer (leichte Flakartillerie) | GUNNER OR OBSERVER (LIGHT AA)
Schütze or Beobachter (leichte Flakartillerie) |

RANGE FINDER OPERATOR (PO COURSE)
Entfernungsmesser (Unteroffizier Lehrgang)

RANGE FINDER OPERATOR WITH AA RANGE FINDER TRAINING
Entfernungsmesser mit Flak-Entfernungsmesser-Messausbildung

RANGE FINDER OPERATOR
Entfernungsmesser

FIRE CONTROLMAN (ARTILLERY, AA, COAST ARTILLERY)
Waffenleitvormann (Artillerie, Flak, Küste)

FIRE CONTROLMAN (SEAMAN TRAINING)
Waffenleitvormann (Truppenausbildung)

MINEMAN (CHIEF)
Sperrvormann

MINEMAN
Sperrmann

TORPEDO FIRE CONTROLMAN II
Torpedo-Waffenleitvormann II

TORPEDO FIRE CONTROLMAN III
Torpedo-Waffenleitvormann III

SUBMARINE AND SALVAGE DIVER
U-Boots- and Bergungs-taucher

TORPEDO DIVER
Torpedo-taucher (Qualified for deeper dives than Ship's Diver)

SHIP'S DIVER
Schiffstaucher

DIVER
Taucher

SOUNDMAN (PO COURSE)
Unterwasserhorcher (Unteroffizierlehrgang)

SOUNDMAN (SEAMAN COURSE)
Unterwasserhorcher (Mannschaftslehrgang)

MOTOR COURSE II
Motorlehrgang II

MOTOR COURSE III
Motorlehrgang III

BANDSMAN
Spielmann

ELECTRICAL COURSE II
Elektrotechnischer Lehrgang II

ELECTRICAL COURSE III
Elektrotechnischer Lehrgang III

TECHNICAL SEARCHLIGHT OPERATOR COURSE (COAST ARTILLERY)
Technischer Scheinwerfer-führer-Lehrgang (Küste)

AA SEARCHLIGHT OPERATOR
Flak-Scheinwerferführer

AA LISTENER (PO COURSE)
Flak-horcher (Unteroffizier-lehrgang)

AA LISTENER (SEAMAN TRAINING)
Flak-horcher (Truppenausbildung)

AA GUN CAPTAIN, COAST ARTILLERY
Flakgeschützführer, Küste

GUN CAPTAIN, COAST ARTILLERY (PO COURSE)
Geschützführer, Küste (Unteroffizierlehrgang)

GUN CAPTAIN, COAST ARTILLERY (SEAMAN TRAINING)
Geschützführer, Küste (Truppenausbildung)

**RATING INSIGNIA:** SEAMAN 1st CLASS, RESTRICTED IN GRADE—Upper left arm.     SEAMAN NON-RESTRICTED—Upper left arm.

These men are beyond the point where they are eligible for promotion to PO and in consequence remain Seamen 1st Class with varying chevrons to indicate their periods of service. Old reserve seamen who have been called to active duty may be placed in this category.

| SEAMAN, 1st CLASS (8 YEARS SERVICE)
Stabsobergefreiter | SEAMAN, 1st CLASS (6 YEARS SERVICE)
Stabsgefreiter | SEAMAN, 1st CLASS (4½ YEARS SERVICE)
Hauptgefreiter | SEAMAN, 1st CLASS
Obergefreiter | SEAMAN 2nd CLASS, AWAITING PROMOTION TO PO
Gefreiter, Unteroffizieranwarter | SEAMAN 2nd CLASS, TAKING PO TRAINING
Gefreiter, Unteroffizierdiensttuer | SEAMAN, 2nd CLASS
Gefreiter |

Apprentice Seamen wear no rating insignia, only their intended Corps Insignia. The Apprentice Seaman is called "Matrose" except: Aircraft Spotter 3rd Class, "Flugmelde"; Naval Artilleryman 3rd Class, "Marineartillerist"; and Ordnanceman 3rd Class, "Feuerwerker".

## PLATE 41

**OFFICERS AND MEN**

**GREEK NAVY**

CAP INSIGNIA, COMMISSIONED AND
WARRANT OFFICERS

CAP FOR FLAG OFFICERS

CAP INSIGNIA, PETTY OFFICERS
Worn with the officer-type cap

**UNIFORMS FOR COMMISSIONED AND
WARRANT OFFICERS**

In addition to the blue (illustrated at left), white,
and khaki—all of which are similar to same U.S.N.
uniforms—there is a heavy weight khaki winter
uniform, similar in cut to the regular khaki but
with khaki colored sleeve stripes instead of
shoulder boards.

**CAP VISORS**

Regulation for Captain through Lieut. Commander, all
Corps; formerly restricted to Line and Engineer Officers.

**UNIFORMS FOR PETTY OFFICERS AND
SEAMEN**

Petty Officers wear blue, white, and khaki uniforms like those worn by British CPO and PO.
These consist of jackets and trousers with officer-
type cap and the insignia illustrated above.

Seamen wear the same blue (illustrated at right),
white, and work jumper-type uniforms as the
British Seamen.

SUBMARINE SERVICE
Ipiresía epí ipovríkhion
(Worn on upper left breast by all submarine personnel)

**OLD ISSUE CAP VISORS, CORPS OFFICERS**
The visors illustrated below may still be seen but are
being replaced by the visor illustrated above.

Legal Officers, Captain through Lieut. Commander

**B NAYTIKON**

SEAMAN CAP BAND
Translation: R(oyal) Navy

BUTTON
Flag Officers

All Other Corps Officers, Captain through Lieut. Commander. (Note: Still worn by Harbor Master Service
Officers)

BUTTON
All personnel below Flag Rank

**LIEUTENANT, LINE**
Ipoplíarkhos
(Blue service uniform. Blue cap cover permitted)

**SEAMAN 1st CLASS, MACHINIST**
Díopos, Mikhanikós
(Blue dress. Blue cap cover permitted)

J.A.N. No. 1
February. 1945
DIVISION OF NAVAL
INTELLIGENCE

PLATE 42

## SHOULDER BOARDS AND SLEEVE INSIGNIA; LINE OFFICERS

GREEK NAVY

| ADMIRAL OF THE FLEET | ADMIRAL | VICE ADMIRAL | REAR ADMIRAL | CAPTAIN | COMMANDER | LIEUTENANT COMMANDER | LIEUTENANT | LIEUTENANT (jg) | ENSIGN |
|---|---|---|---|---|---|---|---|---|---|
| Arkhinávarkhos | Návarkhos | Antinávarkhos | Iponávarkhos | Pliárkhos | Antipliárkhos | Plotárkhis | Ipopliárkhos | Anthipopliárkhos | Simeofóros |
| (Held by the King alone) | (Held by members of the Royal Family only) | | | | | | | | |

## SHOULDER BOARDS AND SLEEVE INSIGNIA; RESERVE AND SPECIAL OFFICERS

CORPS COLORS

RESERVE (Efédros Axiomatikós)—Composed of former Navy regulars and merchant marine personnel. Rank: Captain through Ensign. Corps colors worn between stripes.

VOLUNTEER RESERVE (Epikúros Axiomatikós)—Men with varying professional backgrounds who volunteer for emergency service. Rank: Captain through Ensign. Corps colors worn between stripes.

COMMISSIONED ENLISTED CORPS (Pliromáton Stólu)—Men commissioned from the ranks who wear their former enlisted specialty in gold above loop of rank stripes. Rank: Lieutenant through Ensign. No Corps colors worn.

HARBOR MASTER SERVICE (Limeniki) This service operates in conjunction with the Navy but is under the jurisdiction of the Maritime Service. A gold embroidered anchor worn above straight stripes (no loop) identifies this service. Rank: Captain through Ensign.

| ENSIGN, RESERVE | ENSIGN, VOLUNTEER RESERVE | ENSIGN, MACHINIST, COMMISSIONED ENLISTED CORPS | ENSIGN, HARBOR MASTER SERVICE |
|---|---|---|---|
| Efédros Simeofóros | Epikúros Simeofóros | Simeofóros, Mikhanikós, Pliromáton Stólu | Limenikós Simeofóros |

Corps colors are worn between the stripes on sleeve and shoulder board by Corps Officers of the regular navy, reserve, and volunteer reserve. The method of application follows the British system in all instances.

| (Black) NAVAL CONSTRUCTORS Nafpigi | (Light Violet) ELECTRICAL ENGINEERS Ilektrologi Mikhaniki | (Dark Violet) ENGINEERS Mikhaniki |
| (Lavender) LEGAL OFFICERS Dikastiki | (White) SUPPLY OFFICERS Ikonomiki | (Crimson) DOCTORS Iatrí |
| | | (Green) PHARMACISTS Farmakopii |

## RATING INSIGNIA; WARRANT OFFICERS, PETTY OFFICERS AND SEAMEN

Warrant Officers wear gold stripes on sleeves and shoulder boards as illustrated at right. Petty Officers and Seamen wear chevrons on both upper sleeves; the colors are: gold for Petty Officers, red for Seamen. Apprentice Seaman (Náftis B) and Boy (Naftopés) have no rating insignia.

J.A.N. No. 1
February, 1945
DIVISION OF NAVAL
INTELLIGENCE

| CHIEF WARRANT OFFICER, MACHINIST | WARRANT OFFICER, MACHINIST | CHIEF PETTY OFFICER, MACHINIST | PETTY OFFICER 1st CLASS, MACHINIST | PETTY OFFICER 2nd CLASS, MACHINIST | PETTY OFFICER 3rd CLASS, MACHINIST | SEAMAN 1st CLASS, MACHINIST | SEAMAN 2nd CLASS, MACHINIST |
|---|---|---|---|---|---|---|---|
| Arkhikelefstís A, Mikhanikós | Arkhikelefstís B, Mikhanikós | Kelefstís, Mikhanikós | Ipokelefstís A, Mikhanikós | Ipokelefstís B, Mikhanikós | Dókimos Ipokelefstís, Mikhanikós | Díopos, Mikhanikós | Náftis A, Mikhanikós |

**PLATE 43**

## SPECIALTY INSIGNIA; COMMISSIONED ENLISTED CORPS OFFICERS, AND ALL WARRANT OFFICERS, PETTY OFFICERS AND SEAMEN

**GREEK NAVY**

Color and disposition as follows: Commissioned Enlisted Corps—gold, worn above loop on rank stripes; Warrant Officers—gold, worn above angle on rank stripes; Petty Officers—gold, worn inside rating chevrons on both upper sleeves; Seamen red, worn inside rating chevrons on both upper sleeves except for Apprentice Seamen. The latter, having no rating chevrons, wear their specialty insignia in red, midway between elbow and shoulder on both sleeves.

NOTE: The insignia for the Harbor Master Service is included although this duty comes under the jurisdiction of the Maritime Service, not the Navy.

BOATSWAIN
Armenistis

QUARTERMASTER
Pidaliúkhos

HARBOR MASTER SERVICE
Limenikós

INSTRUCTOR
Ekpedeftis
(Worn above specialty insignia which indicates field of instruction)

MINE MAN
Narkitis

RADARMAN
Radiogoniometritis

SONARMAN
Idrofonitis

TELEGRAPHIST
Tilegrafitis

RADIO ARTIFICER
Tekhnitis Asirmátu

MINE ARTIFICER
Tekhnitis Narkón

LIGHTHOUSE OR SEARCHLIGHT ARTIFICER
Tekhnitis Fáron

GENERAL ARTIFICER
Tekhnitis
(Performs duties of boilermaker, fitter, welder, turner, etc.)

ORDNANCE ARTIFICER (GUNS)
Tekhnitis Pirovólon

TORPEDO ARTIFICER
Tekhnitis Torpillón

ORDNANCE ARTIFICER (EXPLOSIVES)
Tekhnitis Piromakhikón

TORPEDOMAN
Torpillitis

MARKSMAN
Skopeftis

GUNNER
Pirovolitis

FIRE CONTROLMAN
Skopeftis Tilemétron

RANGE FINDER OPERATOR
Tilemetris

DIVER
Ditis

LIGHTHOUSE OR SEARCHLIGHT MAN
Fáron

TELEPHONE MAN
Tilefonitis

COOK
Eskharéfs

STEWARD
Thalamipólos

HOSPITAL CORPSMAN
Nosokómos
(The cross always remains red and the background white. The circle is red for Seamen and gold for all others)

SIGNALMAN
Simatorós

FIREMAN
Thermastis

YEOMAN-STOREKEEPER
Diakhiristis

SHORE PATROL
Oplitis

CARPENTER
Xilurgós

MOTOR MACHINIST
Venzinomikhanikós

MACHINIST
Mikhanikós

ELECTRICIAN
Ilektristis

BUGLER
Salpinktis

MUSICIAN
Musikós

J.A.N. No. 1
February, 1945
DIVISION OF NAVAL INTELLIGENCE

# PLATE 44

## COMMISSIONED OFFICERS

ITALIAN NAVY

CAP

CAP INSIGNIA
Line Officers and Commissioned Enlisted Group

STEEL HELMET

CAP STRIPES

ADMIRAL OF FLEET
Grande Ammiraglio

VICE ADMIRAL
Ammiraglio di Squadra

CAPTAIN
Capitano di Vascello

RANKING LIEUT. AND LIEUT.
1° Tenente e Tenente di Vascello

ADMIRAL
Ammiraglio di Armata

REAR ADMIRAL (Upper Half)
Ammiraglio di Divisione

COMMANDER
Capitano di Fregata

LIEUTENANT (jg)
Sottotenente di Vascello

VICE ADMIRAL (Upper Half)
Ammiraglio Designato di Armata

REAR ADMIRAL
Contrammiraglio

LIEUTENANT COMMANDER
Capitano di Corvetta

ENSIGN
Guardiamarina

CORPS CAP DEVICES

NAVAL
CONSTRUCTORS

NAVAL ORDNANCE

MECHANICAL
ENGINEERS

MEDICAL (DOCTORS)

MEDICAL
(PHARMACISTS)

COMMISSARY

PORT CAPTAINCY

CHAPLAINS

COMMANDER, LINE, (PILOT OFFICER)
Capitano di Fregata, Stato Maggiore,
(Ufficiale Pilota)

LAPEL STAR

PILOT OFFICERS
Ufficiali Piloti

SUBMARINE OFFICERS
Ufficiali Imbarcati su Sommergibili

OBSERVER OFFICERS
Ufficiali Osservatori

BUTTON
Senior and Junior Officers

LIEUTENANT COMMANDER, LINE
Capitano di Corvetta,
Stato Maggiore

J.A.N. No. 1: APRIL 1943

# PLATE 45

**SHOULDER INSIGNIA**—For Blue Uniform Only.   COMMISSIONED OFFICERS

| ADMIRALS<br>Line | NAVAL CONSTRUCTORS<br>Flag Officers | NAVAL ORDNANCE<br>Flag Officers | MEDICAL<br>Flag Officers | COMMISSARY<br>Flag Officers | PORT CAPTAINCY<br>Flag Officers | SENIOR OFFICERS<br>Captains to Ranking Lieutenants | JUNIOR OFFICERS<br>Lieutenants to Ensigns |
|---|---|---|---|---|---|---|---|

## SLEEVE INSIGNIA

Only Line Officers wear loop. Other Corps use appropriate colors as background for stripes on cap and sleeve, as edging of shoulder boards and shoulder insignia, and as background of cap insignia. The Commissioned Enlisted Group have neither corps color nor loop but wear special insignia above sleeve stripes. NOTE: Medical Corps (Doctors) color is always turquoise, except as background for cap device, where it is white.

| ADMIRAL OF FLEET<br>Grande Ammiraglio | ADMIRAL<br>Ammiraglio di Armata | VICE ADMIRAL (Upper Half)<br>Ammiraglio Designato di Armata | VICE ADMIRAL<br>Ammiraglio di Squadra | REAR ADMIRAL (Upper Half)<br>Ammiraglio di Divisione | REAR ADMIRAL<br>Contrammiraglio |
|---|---|---|---|---|---|

| CAPTAIN<br>Capitano di Vascello | COMMANDER<br>Capitano di Fregata | LIEUTENANT COMMANDER<br>Capitano di Corvetta | RANKING LIEUT AND LIEUT<br>1° Tenente e Tenente di Vascello | LIEUTENANT (jg)<br>Sottotenente di Vascello | ENSIGN<br>Guardiamarina |
|---|---|---|---|---|---|

## SHOULDER INSIGNIA

**SPECIALTY INSIGNIA**—COMMISSIONED ENLISTED GROUP

| ADMIRAL OF FLEET<br>Grande Ammiraglio | ADMIRAL<br>Ammiraglio di Armata | VICE ADMIRAL (Upper Half)<br>Ammiraglio Designato di Armata | VICE ADMIRAL<br>Ammiraglio di Squadra | REAR ADMIRAL (Upper Half)<br>Ammiraglio di Divisione | REAR ADMIRAL<br>Contrammiraglio |
|---|---|---|---|---|---|

Commissioned from ranks. Worn just above sleeve stripes. Duties similar to U.S. Warrant Officers. Rank extends from Ensign to Lieutenant, bearing Army titles.

 NAUTICAL SERVICES<br>Servizi Nautici

| REAR ADMIRAL (Upper Half)<br>Naval Constructors | REAR ADMIRAL (Upper Half)<br>Naval Ordnance | REAR ADMIRAL (Upper Half)<br>Medical | REAR ADMIRAL (Upper Half)<br>Commissary | REAR ADMIRAL (Upper Half)<br>Port Captaincy | CAPTAIN<br>Capitano di Vascello |
|---|---|---|---|---|---|

TECHNICAL SERVICES<br>Servizi Tecnici

MACHINERY SERVICES<br>Servizi Macchina

| COMMANDER<br>Capitano di Fregata | LIEUTENANT COMMANDER<br>Capitano di Corvetta | RANKING LIEUTENANT<br>1° Tenente di Vascello | LIEUTENANT<br>Tenente di Vascello | LIEUTENANT (jg)<br>Sottotenente di Vascello | ENSIGN<br>Guardiamarina |
|---|---|---|---|---|---|

ACCOUNTANCY SERVICES<br>Servizi Contabili

DIRECTORS OF MUSICAL CORPS<br>Direttori del Corpo Musicale

J.A.N. No. 1<br>February, 1945<br>DIVISION OF NAVAL<br>INTELLIGENCE

PLATE 46

**PETTY OFFICERS**

**ITALIAN NAVY**

CHIEF PETTY OFFICER, 1st CLASS, YEOMAN
Capo 1ª Classe, Furiere

SHOULDER BOARDS (Worn by Chief Petty Officers on white uniform)

CHIEF PETTY OFFICER, 1st CLASS, YEOMAN
Capo 1ª Classe, Furiere

CHIEF PETTY OFFICER, 2nd CLASS, FIREMAN
Capo 2ª Classe, Fuochista

CHIEF PETTY OFFICER, 3rd CLASS, SIGNALMAN
Capo 3ª Classe, Segnalatore

CAP INSIGNIA

RANK STRIPES
WORN ON UPPER SLEEVES
OF BLUE AND WHITE UNIFORMS

PETTY OFFICER (UPPER HALF), HOSPITAL CORPSMAN
Secondo Capo, Infermiere

PETTY OFFICER (LOWER HALF), GUNNER
Sergente, Cannoniere

BUTTON

LAPEL STAR

RANK INSIGNIA (Worn by Chief Petty Officer; sewn on shoulders of blue uniform)

CHIEF PETTY OFFICER, 1st CLASS
Capo 1ª Classe

CHIEF PETTY OFFICER, 2nd CLASS
Capo 2ª Classe

CHIEF PETTY OFFICER, 3rd CLASS
Capo 3ª Classe

PETTY OFFICER (LOWER HALF), GUNNER
Sergente, Cannoniere
(Sergente is a new rating)

J.A.N. No. 1:  APRIL 1943

# PLATE 47

**SPECIALTY INSIGNIA** – Worn by Chief Petty Officer on both sleeves about 3 inches above cuff of blue uniform and on shoulder boards; by other Petty Officers above vertex of rank stripes on blue and white uniforms.    **ITALIAN NAVY**

| | | | | | | | |
|---|---|---|---|---|---|---|---|
| QUARTERMASTERS<br>Nocchieri |  SIGNALMEN<br>Segnalatori |  ELECTRICIAN'S MATES<br>Elettricisti |  AIDES<br>Aiutanti |  CARPENTER'S MATES<br>Carpentieri |  DAMAGE CONTROL MEN<br>Destinati ai Parchi Pompieri |  RADIOMEN<br>Radiotelegrafisti |  TORPEDOMAN'S MATES<br>Siluristi |
|  MINE MEN<br>Torpedinieri | 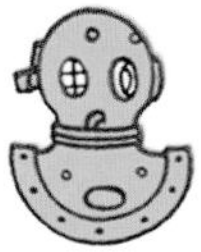 DIVERS<br>Palombari | 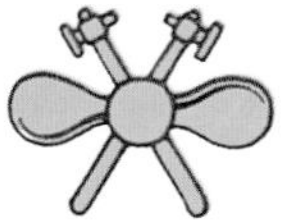 MACHINIST'S MATES<br>Meccanici |  YEOMEN<br>Furieri |  COMMISSARY STEWARDS<br>Furieri (Sussistenza) | 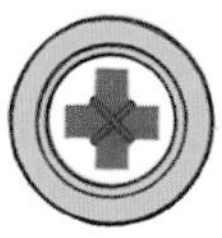 HOSPITAL CORPSMEN<br>Infermieri |  FIREMEN<br>Fuochisti |  MUSICIANS<br>Musicanti |
|  BUGLERS<br>Trombettieri |  PORT CORPS<br>Portuali | 1st CLASS RANGE FINDER OPERATORS<br>Cannonieri Telemetristi di 1a Classe | 2nd CLASS RANGE FINDER OPERATORS<br>Cannonieri Telemetristi di 2a Classe | 1st CLASS STEREO-RANGE FINDER OPERATORS<br>Cannonieri Stereotelemetristi di 1a Classe | 2nd CLASS STEREO-RANGE FINDER OPERATORS<br>Cannonieri Stereotelemetristi di 2a Classe |  EXPERT GUN POINTERS AT CENTRAL STATION<br>Cannonieri Puntatori Scelti Centrali |  GUN POINTERS<br>Cannonieri Puntatori |
|  GUNNERS<br>Cannonieri |  EXPERT MACHINE GUNNERS<br>Cannonieri Puntatori Scelti Mitraglieri |  ORDNANCE REPAIRMEN<br>Cannonieri Armaroli |  CHIEF FIRE CONTROL MEN AT CENTRAL STATION<br>Specialisti Direzione Tiro Capi Centrale |  FIRE CONTROL MEN<br>Specialisti Direzione Tiro | DEEP SEA DIVERS<br>Palombari di Grande Profondità | HYDROPHONE OPERATORS<br>Idrofonisti | COMPASS READERS<br>Conduttori di Girobussole |
| COMPASS MOUNTERS<br>Montatori di Girobussole |  SPECIALISTS WITH MOUNTER'S LICENSE<br>Specialisti con Brevetto di Montatori |  SUBMARINE PERSONNEL<br>Imbarcati su Sommergibili |  PROMOTION FOR WAR MERIT<br>Promozione per Merito di Guerra | DEGREE RECEIVED<br>Laureati | DIPLOMA RECEIVED<br>Diplomati |  ATHLETIC INSTRUCTORS<br>Istruttori di Educazione Fisica |  FENCING INSTRUCTORS<br>Istruttori di Scherma |

J.A.N. No. 1;<br>APRIL 1943<br>ITALIAN NAVY

PLATE 48

**SEAMEN**

**ITALIAN NAVY**

CAP
In White for Summer Uniform

RANK INSIGNIA
Worn on Both Upper Sleeves

**LEADING SEAMAN**
Sottocapo

**1st CLASS SEAMAN**
Funzionante Sottocapo

**2nd CLASS SEAMAN**
Comune di 1ª Classe

**LEADING SEAMAN, QUARTERMASTER**
Sottocapo, Nocchiere
Winter Uniform

**WINTER FATIGUE UNIFORM**

SERVICE CAP

**SQUADRON INSIGNIA**
Directly Below Left Shoulder Seam

| SEAMAN BRANCH | OTHER BRANCHES |
|---|---|
| White on Blue Uniform | Red on Blue Uniform |
| Red on White Uniform | Blue on White Uniform |

**FIRST SQUADRON**
Prima Squadra

**SECOND SQUADRON**
Seconda Squadra

**THIRD SQUADRON**
Terza Squadra

**FOURTH SQUADRON**
Quarta Squadra

**1st CLASS SEAMAN, TORPEDOMAN**
Funzionante Sottocapo, Silurista
Summer Dress Uniform

J.A.N. No. 1: APRIL 1943

# PLATE 49

## SEAMEN SPECIALTY INSIGNIA
Worn above Vertex of Rank Insignia

**ITALIAN NAVY**
J.A.N. No 1   APRIL 1943

| | | | |
|---|---|---|---|
|  **QUARTERMASTERS** Nocchieri |  **DRAFTED APPRENTICE SEAMEN** Marinai di Leva |  **SIGNALMEN** Segnalatori |  **DIVERS** Palombari |
|  **HOSPITAL CORPSMEN** Infermieri |  **GUNNERS** Cannonieri |  | |

| | | |
|---|---|---|
|  **1st CLASS RANGE FINDER OPERATORS** Cannonieri Telemetristi di 1ª Classe |  **2nd CLASS RANGE FINDER OPERATORS** Cannonieri Telemetristi di 2ª Classe |  **1st CLASS STEREO-RANGE FINDER OPERATORS** Cannonieri Stereotelemetristi di 1ª Classe |
|  **2nd CLASS STEREO-RANGE FINDER OPERATORS** Cannonieri Stereotelemetristi di 2ª Classe |  **EXPERT GUN POINTERS** Cannonieri Puntatori Scelti |  **EXPERT GUN POINTERS AT CENTRAL STATION** Cannonieri Puntatori Scelti Centrali |
|  **ORDNANCE ARTIFICERS** Cannonieri Artificieri |  **MACHINE GUNNERS** Cannonieri Puntatori Mitraglieri |  **ORDNANCE REPAIRMEN** Cannonieri Armaroli |

| | | |
|---|---|---|
|  **FIRE CONTROLMEN (VOLUNTEER)** Specialisti Direzione Tiro (Volontari) |  **FIRE CONTROLMEN (DRAFTED)** Specialisti Direzione Tiro (di Leva) |  **RADIOMEN** Radiotelegrafisti |
|  **ELECTRICIANS** Elettricisti |  **TORPEDOMEN** Siluristi |  **MINEMEN** Torpedinieri |
|  **MACHINISTS** Meccanici |  **YEOMEN** Furieri Ordinari |  **COMMISSARY STEWARDS** Furieri Sussistenza |

| | | |
|---|---|---|
|  **ARTIFICER FIREMEN** Fuochisti Artefici |  **ORDINARY FIREMEN** Fuochisti Ordinari |  **ARTIFICER FIREMEN (MOTOR SPECIALISTS)** Fuochisti Artefici Motoristi Abilitati |
|  **ORDINARY FIREMEN (MOTOR SPECIALISTS)** Fuochisti Ordinari Motoristi Abilitati |  **ARTIFICER FIREMEN (MARINE MOTORS) VOLUNTEER** Fuochisti Artefici Motoristi Navali Volontari |  **ARTIFICER FIREMEN (MARINE MOTORS) DRAFTED** Fuochisti Artefici Motoristi Navali di Leva |
|  **ARTIFICER FIREMEN (ENGINEERS) VOLUNTEER** Fuochisti Artefici Macchinari Volontari |  **ARTIFICER FIREMEN (ENGINEERS) DRAFTED** Fuochisti Artefici Macchinari di Leva |  **ORDINARY FIREMEN (ENGINEERS)** Fuochisti Ordinari Macchinari |

| | | |
|---|---|---|
|  **SUBMARINE PERSONNEL** Personale Imbarcato su Sommergibili |  **CARPENTERS** Carpentieri |  **DAMAGE CONTROLMEN** Pompieri |
|  **MUSICIANS** Musicanti |  **BUGLERS** Trombettieri |  **PORT CORPS** Portuali |
|  **LEADING SEAMEN ELIGIBLE FOR PETTY OFFICER** Sottocapi Brevettati Secondi Capi Worn above cuff |  **VOLUNTEERS** Volontari Worn above cuff |  **LICENSED MOUNTERS** Brevettati Montatori |

| | | |
|---|---|---|
|  **CHAUFFEURS** Autisti |  **SERVICE STRIPES, LEADING SEAMEN (VOLUNTEER)** Sottocapi Volontari Worn above cuff |  **SERVICE STRIPES, DRAFTED SEAMEN** Militari di Leva Worn above cuff |
|  **COMPASS READERS** Conduttori Girobussole |  **DEEP SEA DIVERS** Palombari di Grande Profondità |  **HIGH SCHOOL GRADUATE** Titolo di Studio |
|  **DIPLOMA RECEIVED** Diplomati |  **HYDROPHONE OPERATORS** Idrofonisti | **L** **DEGREE RECEIVED** Laureati |

PLATE 50

**COMMISSIONED OFFICERS**

LIEUTENANT COMMANDER, LINE
Shōsa

LINE OFFICER'S CAP
Corps Officers wear Corps color piping on bottom of cap at back

OFFICER'S BUTTON

FIELD CAP, ALL PERSONNEL
Also in white and (for Marines) in khaki

CAP INSIGNIA, MIDSHIPMEN AND CADETS, LINE
Anchor is in Corps color for Corps personnel

CAP INSIGNIA, ALL OFFICERS

FIELD CAP AND HELMET INSIGNIA, ALL PERSONNEL, OLD STYLE
Also on Marine's mobile equipment

SHOULDER BOARD, LIEUTENANT COMMANDER, LINE

COLLAR PATCH, LIEUTENANT, MEDICAL CORPS

**CORPS COLORS.** Line Officers have no Corps color; all others, below flag rank, use Corps colors illustrated below. Corps Flag Officers are indistinguishable from Line. Colors appear on shoulder boards, on collar patches, at back of cap, and on anchor in Midshipman and Cadet's cap. Color as background for sleeve stripes appears only with the dress uniform.

| TECHNICAL Gijutsu | AVIATION Kōkū | AVIATION ENGINEERING, MAINTENANCE Seibi | MEDICAL; PHARMACY Gun-i; Yakuzai | PAYMASTER Shukei | MUSIC Gungaku |

LIEUTENANT, MEDICAL CORPS
Gun-i Tai-i
(Long sword is carried in active combat)

**PLATE 51**

## COLLAR, SHOULDER, SLEEVE INSIGNIA; COMMISSIONED OFFICERS

**JAPANESE NAVY**

Insignia of rank as seen in collar patch, shoulder board and sleeve stripe is illustrated at right and below, each unit following the order of collar, shoulder, and sleeve from top to bottom. Collar patches and sleeve stripes illustrated are as worn on left arm and collar, shoulder boards are as worn on right shoulder. Sleeve stripes are worn only on the blue uniform. On the service blue of wartime wear the stripes are black, but for clarity in reproduction they have been illustrated here in gold, just as they would appear on the dress blue uniform. Collar patches are worn only on the service blue uniform and on the Marine's khaki uniform. Shoulder boards are worn only on the white uniform and on the overcoat.

ADMIRAL
Taishō

VICE ADMIRAL
Chūshō or Chūjō

REAR ADMIRAL
Shōshō

CAPTAIN
Taisa

COMMANDER
Chūsa

LIEUTENANT COMMANDER
Shōsa

LIEUTENANT
Tai-i

LIEUTENANT (jg)
Chū-i

ENSIGN
Shō-i

MIDSHIPMAN
Shō-i Kōhosei

CADET
Seito

WARRANT OFFICER
Jun-i

## SLEEVE INSIGNIA; NAVAL RESERVE

## SHOULDER AND COLLAR INSIGNIA; CORPS

Naval Reserve Officers are recruited largely from the Merchant Marine. When called to active duty they drop their reserve status and change to regulation Navy insignia. Reserve Officers are rare in wartime, but some may be met in merchant ships independent of the Navy. Captain is the highest rank, and the number of stripes for each grade corresponds to regulation Japanese Navy practice.

LIEUTENANT COMMANDER,
NAVAL RESERVE
Yobi Shōsa

Shoulder

LIEUTENANT COMMANDER,
AVIATION CORPS
Kōkū Shōsa

Shoulder

ENSIGN, MEDICAL CORPS
Gun-i Shō-i

Collar

COMMANDER, TECHNICAL CORPS
Gijutsu Chūsa

Collar

LIEUTENANT (jg), PAYMASTER'S CORPS
Shukei Chū-i

J.A.N. No. 1:
SEPTEMBER 1943

PLATE 52

## COMMISSIONED OFFICERS

## JAPANESE NAVY

SWORD. Officers only. Variation exists in decoration of scabbard and hilt. Used during active duty as symbol of authority.

FIGHTER PILOT
High on left sleeve.
Blue on white uniform.

NAVAL ENSIGN. Used as flag or insignia to identify Navy vessels, troops (Marines), equipment. Army uses white flag with red circle for same purpose.

BOMBER PILOT
High on left sleeve.
Blue on white uniform.

### CAPE COLLAR INSIGNIA

FLAG OFFICERS
Shōkan
(Adm., Vice Adm., Rear Adm.)

SENIOR OFFICERS
Sakan
(Capt., Lt. Comdr., Comdr.)

JUNIOR OFFICERS
Ikan
(Lt., Lt. (jg), Ens.)

LIEUTENANT (jg), MARINE
Chū-i, Rikusentai
(Summer field dress; helmet cover)

ENSIGN, MARINE
Sho-i, Rikusentai
(Tropical; leather puttees or boots optional)

MARINES (Rikusentai). Strictly speaking, the Japanese have no Marine "Corps"; anyone in Navy may be detached from regular shipboard duties for landing and policing operations. However, the need for large numbers of men for such duty means that a "Corps" performing Marine functions exists in fact, though from an administrative viewpoint they remain regular Navy personnel. Except for use of Navy insignia, Marine uniform for Officers and Men is same as that now used by Army; but enormous individual variation may be expected. Lapel insignia now supersede shoulder boards or Navy insignia on shoulder straps. Gold anchors on shoulders may distinguish Petty Officers. Some units may even use Army rank insignia. The least variable identifying features are gold anchor on cap or helmet and Navy flag which is carried in battle and which marks Marine mobile shore equipment.

PLATE 53

# PETTY OFFICERS AND SEAMEN

SUPERIOR PETTY OFFICER, BOATSWAIN

Joto Heiso
(Advanced Special Training.
Good Conduct Chevrons)

EXTRA AND ADVANCED SPECIAL TRAINING
Upper left sleeve

## INSIGNIA; NEW STYLE

For Petty Officers and Seamen; Marines (naval landing units) presumably also use this new insignia. Rating insignia is yellow for all uniforms, and the background is the same color as the uniform. Within each rating device is a cherry blossom which by its color indicates the Corps. Yellow chevrons indicate Good Conduct. Special Training is now shown by just two devices: one for Elementary (Futsuka), the other for both Advanced (Kotoka) and Extra (Tokushuka). Again the color is yellow for all uniforms. Nomenclature of rating has also been changed; the new titles are used here throughout except under illustrations of the older designs.

ELEMENTARY SPECIAL TRAINING
Upper left sleeve

**CORPS COLORS,** NEW STYLE—These appear above anchor as part of Rating Insignia, upper right sleeve.

| SEAMAN BRANCH | AVIATION | AVIATION MAINTENANCE | ENGINEERING; CON- | HOSPITAL CORPS | PAYMASTER | MUSIC |
| Sui Hei | Kōkū or Hikō | Seibi | STRUCTION AND REPAIR | Eisei or Kango | Shukei | Gungaku |
| | | | Kikan; Kōsaku | | | |

**RATING INSIGNIA,** NEW STYLE---Worn on upper right sleeve.

| SUPERIOR PETTY OFFICER | PETTY OFFICER, 1st CLASS | PETTY OFFICER, 2nd CLASS | LEADING SEAMAN | SUPERIOR SEAMAN | SEAMAN, 1st CLASS | SEAMAN, 2nd CLASS |
| Jōtō Heisō | Ittō Heisō | Nitō Heisō | Heichō | Jōtō Hei | Ittō Hei | Nitō Hei |
| (Seaman Branch) | (Aviation) | (Aviation Maintenance) | (Engineering) | (Hospital Corps) | (Paymaster) | (Musician) |

PETTY OFFICER 2nd CLASS, ENGINEER

Nitō Kikan Heisō
(Elementary Special Training.
Good Conduct Chevron)

J.A.N. No. 1: SEPTEMBER 1943

# PLATE 54

**PETTY OFFICERS AND SEAMEN**

**JAPANESE NAVY**

SEAMAN'S DRESS CAP

大日本帝國海軍

CAP BAND FOR ALL SEAMEN

**FIGHTER PILOT**
High on left sleeve.
(Blue on white uniform)

**PETTY OFFICER'S
CAP INSIGNIA**

**BOMBER PILOT**
High on left sleeve.
(Blue on white uniform)

**PETTY OFFICER'S
BUTTON**

**SEAMAN'S BUTTON**

**CONDUCT CHEVRONS**
Right sleeve. Old style are
red on blue uniform, blue
on white; "Excellent Con-
duct" has gold blossom.

**EXCELLENT CONDUCT**

**GOOD CONDUCT**

**MARINE'S SERVICE CAP**
All ranks. Also in blue and white for all sea-
going personnel.

**SEAMAN, FATIGUE UNIFORM**
Also worn by P.O.

**LEADING SEAMAN, SEAMAN BRANCH**
Heicho
(Good Conduct Chevron. Shore rig)

**SUPERIOR SEAMAN, HOSPITAL CORPS**
Jōtō Eisei Hei

**MARINE**
Rikusentai
(Seaman 1st Class)

J A N. No. 1
SEPTEMBER 1943

PLATE 55

**SPECIAL TRAINING INSIGNIA, OLD STYLE; PETTY OFFICERS AND SEAMEN** — Upper left sleeve.

J.A.N. No. 1. SEPTEMBER 1943 **JAPANESE NAVY**

## SPECIAL TRAINING INSIGNIA

Of the three degrees of Special Training, Elementary is taken mostly by Seamen before becoming Petty Officers, Advanced is mainly for Petty Officers, and Extra is entirely for Petty Officers. Insignia is light blue when on white uniform.

## RATING INSIGNIA

Corps, or branch of service, within each rating is distinguished by difference in central design rather than in color. The insignia is light blue when worn on the white uniform. Seaman 4th Class wears no insignia.

*Old Style Special Training and Rating Insignia have been abolished since November, 1942, but may still be encountered in outlying posts. See accompanying pages for New Style Insignia and new titles of rank for Petty Officers and Seamen.*

### GUNNERY
Hō

EXTRA    ADVANCED    ELEMENTARY

### MUSIC
Gungaku

EXTRA

### SEAMANSHIP
Unyō

ADVANCED    ELEMENTARY

### TORPEDOES
Suirai

ADVANCED    ELEMENTARY

### MINES
Kirai

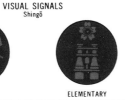 

ADVANCED    ELEMENTARY

### FIRE CONTROL
Sokuteki

ADVANCED    ELEMENTARY

### CONSTRUCTION AND REPAIR
Kōsaku

EXTRA    ADVANCED    ELEMENTARY

### VISUAL SIGNALS
Shingō

ADVANCED    ELEMENTARY

### AVIATION
Kōkū

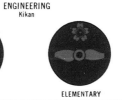 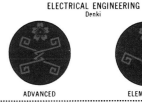 

NAVIGATOR    PILOT OR OBSERVER    AVIATION TRAINING

### AVIATION ENGINEERING
Kōkū Seibi

ADVANCED    ELEMENTARY

### AVIATION ORDNANCE
Kōkū Heiki

ADVANCED    ELEMENTARY

### ENGINEERING
Kikan

ADVANCED    ELEMENTARY

### ELECTRICAL ENGINEERING
Denki

ADVANCED    ELEMENTARY

### TELEGRAPHY
Denshin

ADVANCED    ELEMENTARY

### HOSPITAL CORPS
Eisei

ADVANCED    ELEMENTARY

### ACCOUNTING
Shukei

ADVANCED    ELEMENTARY

### SUPPLY
Iryō

ADVANCED    ELEMENTARY

PLATE 56

**RATING INSIGNIA, OLD STYLE; PETTY OFFICERS AND SEAMEN** — Upper Right Sleeve.

| | SEAMAN BRANCH | AVIATION | AVIATION MAINTENANCE | ENGINEERING | CONSTRUCTION AND REPAIR | HOSPITAL CORPS | PAYMASTER | MUSIC |
|---|---|---|---|---|---|---|---|---|
| PETTY OFFICER, 1st CLASS<br>Ittō Heisō<br>(New, Superior P.O.) |  | | | | | | | |
| PETTY OFFICER, 2nd CLASS<br>Nitō Heisō<br>(New, P.O., 1st Class) | 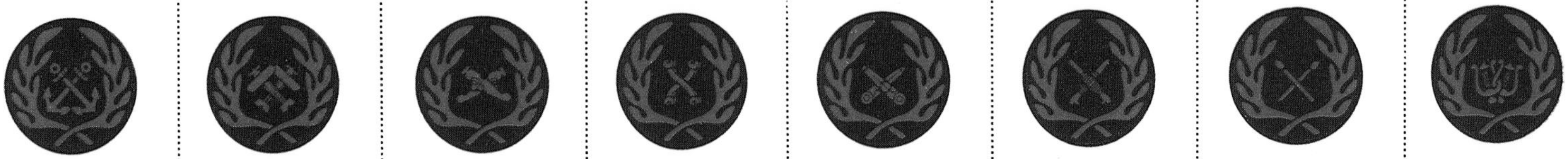 | | | | | | | |
| PETTY OFFICER, 3rd CLASS<br>Santō Heisō<br>(New, P.O., 2nd Class) | 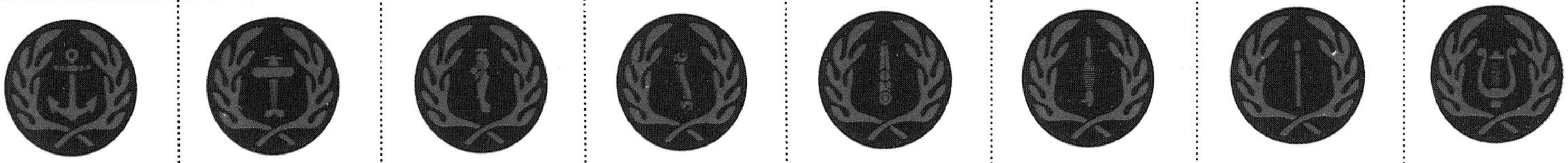 | | | | | | | |
| SEAMAN, 1st CLASS<br>Ittō Hei<br>(New, Leading Seaman) | 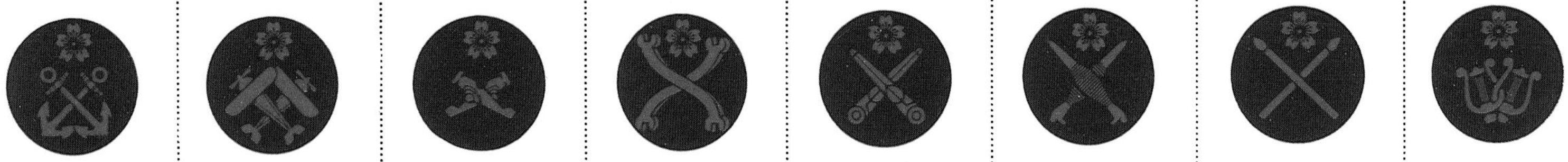 | | | | | | | |
| SEAMAN, 2nd CLASS<br>Nitō Hei<br>(New, Superior Seaman) |  | | | | | | | |
| SEAMAN, 3rd CLASS<br>Santō Hei<br>(New, Seaman 1st Class) | 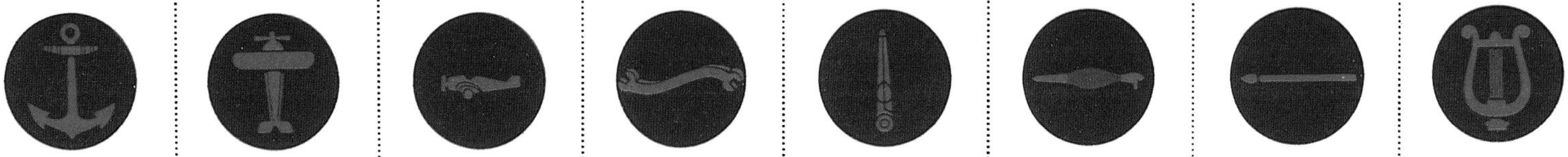 | | | | | | | |

# PLATE 57

## COMMISSIONED OFFICERS

## ROYAL NETHERLANDS NAVY

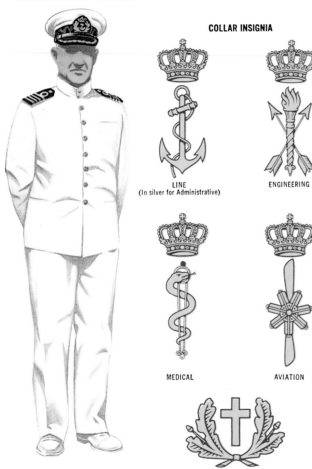

**CAPTAIN, LINE**
Kapitein ter Zee

### COLLAR INSIGNIA

**LINE**
(In silver for Administrative)

**ENGINEERING**

**MEDICAL**

**AVIATION**

**CHAPLAINS**

**LIEUTENANT COMMANDER, LINE**
Luitenant ter Zee 1e Klasse

**TROPICAL HELMET**

### BUTTONS

**LINE, AVIATION, AND CHAPLAINS**

**ADMINISTRATIVE**

**ENGINEERING**

**MEDICAL**

### SPECIAL SERVICE INSIGNIA

**SD**

Worn inside the loop of sleeve stripe and shoulder board by Special Service Officers (Officieren voor Speciale Diensten). These are Reserve Officers who have been called to service for special duty. They may hold rank from Captain to Ensign.

**ENSIGN, LINE**
Luitenant ter Zee 3e Klasse
(Tropical uniform. Similar uniform in khaki for fatigue wear)

J.A.N. No 1: OCTOBER 1943

PLATE 58

# SHOULDER BOARDS AND SLEEVE INSIGNIA; COMMISSIONED OFFICERS—Silver stripes for Administrative Officers

ROYAL NETHERLANDS NAVY

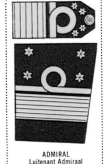

| ADMIRAL<br>Luitenant Admiraal | VICE ADMIRAL<br>Vice Admiraal | REAR ADMIRAL<br>Schout-bij-Nacht | CAPTAIN<br>Kapitein ter Zee | COMMANDER<br>Kapitein-Luitenant ter Zee | LIEUTENANT COMMANDER<br>Luitenant ter Zee 1e Klasse | LIEUTENANT<br>Luitenant ter Zee 2e Klasse | ENSIGN<br>Luitenant ter Zee 3e Klasse | CHAPLAIN<br>Vloot Geestelijke<br>(Ranks between Lieutenant Commander and Commander) |

## CAP INSIGNIA

| LINE<br>Zee Officieren | AVIATION<br>Officieren-Vlieger | ENGINEERING<br>Officieren van den Marine-Stoomvaartdienst | MEDICAL<br>Officieren van Gezondheid | ADMINISTRATIVE<br>Officieren van Administratie | CHAPLAINS<br>Vloot Geestlijken |

## AVIATION INSIGNIA — Worn on left breast.

| PILOT-OBSERVER<br>Vlieger-Waarnemer | PILOT<br>Vlieger | OBSERVER<br>Waarnemer | AIR TELEGRAPHIST-GUNNER<br>Vliegtuig Telegrafist Schutter | AIR GUNNER<br>Vliegtuig Schutter | AIR TELEGRAPHIST<br>Vliegtuig Telegrafist |

J.A.N. No. 1:<br>OCTOBER 1943

# PLATE 59

## WARRANT AND PETTY OFFICERS

## ROYAL NETHERLANDS NAVY

CAP; WINTER WEAR

**CAP INSIGNIA**

For all specialties
except Musician.
In silver for Yeomen.

For Musicians

### AVIATION INSIGNIA
Worn on left breast

PILOT
Vlieger

OBSERVER
Waarnemer

AIR TELEGRAPHIST GUNNER
Vliegtuig Telegrafist Schutter

AIR GUNNER
Vliegtuigschutter

AIR TELEGRAPHIST
Vliegtuig Telegrafist

**WARRANT OFFICER**
Adjudant-onderofficier
(Tropical uniform; specialty insignia never worn)

**CHIEF PETTY OFFICER, BOATSWAIN**
Schnipper

### RATING INSIGNIA
In silver for Yeomen

#### WARRANT OFFICER
Warrant Machinist is called Adjudant-onderofficier-
machinist; Warrant Pilot is called Adjudant-onder-
officier-vlieger; Warrants of all other specialties are
called Opper plus the specialty name.

SLEEVE
Blue uniform

SHOULDER
White and tropical uniforms

#### CHIEF PETTY OFFICER
C.P.O., Boatswain, is called Schipper; for all other
specialties, Majoor plus specialty name.

SLEEVE
Blue uniform

COLLAR
White and tropical uniforms

#### PETTY OFFICER, 1st CLASS
P.O. 1st Class, Boatswain, is called Bootsman; for all
other specialties, Sergeant plus specialty name.

SLEEVE
Blue uniform

COLLAR
White and tropical uniforms

**PETTY OFFICER, 1st CLASS**
Sergeant
(Specialty insignia never worn on this uniform)

J.A.N. No. I: OCTOBER 1943

PLATE 60

**SEAMEN**

STRAW HAT
Worn in East Indies. Old style cap band.

CAP
Worn with white cover for summer

## KONINKLIJKE MARINE

CAP BAND
New style

**RATING INSIGNIA; LEADING SEAMAN**
In white for Yoeman. Leading Seaman, with specialty of Boatswain, is called Kwartiermeester; for all other specialties, Korporaal plus the name of the specialty.

Worn on overcoat

Worn on jumper-type and
tropical uniforms

LEADING SEAMAN, BOATSWAIN
Kwartiermeester
(Blue uniform with overcoat)

LEADING SEAMAN, BOATSWAIN
Kwartiermeester
(Summer uniform)

TROPICAL UNIFORM
Specialty insignia never worn. Only Leading
Seaman wears rating insignia.

SEAMAN 2nd CLASS, BOATSWAIN
Matroos 2e Klasse
(Winter uniform)

J.A.N. No. 1: OCTOBER 1943

PLATE 61

## SPECIALTY INSIGNIA; WARRANT AND PETTY OFFICERS — Upper left sleeve of blue uniform.

| SIGNALMAN Seiner | TELEGRAPHIST Telegrafist | BOATSWAIN SERVICE Bootsmansvak | ORDNANCE REPAIRMAN Konstabel | TORPEDOMAN Torpedomaker | FIRE CONTROLMAN Geschutmaker | ELECTRICIAN Monteur | MACHINIST Machinist |

| CARPENTER Timmerman | AVIATION REPAIRMAN Vliegtuigmaker | PILOT Vlieger | YEOMAN Schrijver | STEWARD; COOK Hofmeester; Kok | HOSPITAL CORPSMAN Ziekenverpleger | STOREKEEPER Bottelier | MUSICIAN Stafmuzikant |

## SPECIAL SERVICE INSIGNIA; SEAMEN — Worn on upper right sleeve of blue uniform.

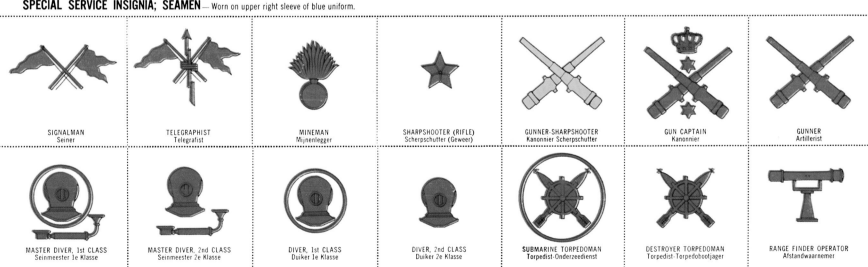

| SIGNALMAN Seiner | TELEGRAPHIST Telegrafist | MINEMAN Mijnenlegger | SHARPSHOOTER (RIFLE) Scherpschutter (Geweer) | GUNNER-SHARPSHOOTER Kanonnier Scherpschutter | GUN CAPTAIN Kanonnier | GUNNER Artillerist |

| MASTER DIVER, 1st CLASS Seinmeester 1e Klasse | MASTER DIVER, 2nd CLASS Seinmeester 2e Klasse | DIVER, 1st CLASS Duiker 1e Klasse | DIVER, 2nd CLASS Duiker 2e Klasse | SUBMARINE TORPEDOMAN Torpedist-Onderzeedienst | DESTROYER TORPEDOMAN Torpedist-Torpedobootjager | RANGE FINDER OPERATOR Afstandwaarnemer |

J.A.N. No. 1:
OCTOBER 1943

PLATE 62

## SPECIALTY INSIGNIA; SEAMEN — Worn on upper left sleeve.

ROYAL NETHERLANDS NAVY

On the blue uniform and the overcoat, specialty insignia are worn by all Seamen. On the white jumper-type uniform, these insignia are worn by all Seamen except the Leading Seaman. On the tropical uniform specialty insignia is never worn.

**LEADING SEAMAN AND SEAMAN
1st CLASS, SIGNALMAN**
Korporaal Seiner and Seinersmaat

**LEADING SEAMAN AND SEAMAN
1st CLASS, TELEGRAPHIST**
Korporaal Telegrafist and
Telegrafistenmaat

**LEADING SEAMAN, BOATSWAIN**
Kwartiermeester

**SEAMAN 1st CLASS, BOATSWAIN**
Matroos 1e Klasse

**SEAMAN 2nd CLASS, BOATSWAIN**
Matroos 2e Klasse

**LEADING SEAMAN AND SEAMAN
1st CLASS, ORDNANCE REPAIRMAN**
Korporaal Konstabel and
Konstabelsmaat

**LEADING SEAMAN AND SEAMAN
1st CLASS, TORPEDOMAN**
Korporaal Torpedomaker and
Torpedomakersmaat

**APPRENTICE TORPEDOMAN,
3rd YEAR**
Leerling Torpedomaker, 3e Jaar
(Open to Seaman 1st Class only)

**APPRENTICE TORPEDOMAN,
2nd YEAR**
Leerling Torpedomaker, 2e Jaar
(Open to Seaman 2nd Class only)

**APPRENTICE TORPEDOMAN,
1st YEAR**
Leerling Torpedomaker, 1e Jaar
(Open to Apprentice Seaman only)

**LEADING SEAMAN AND SEAMAN
1st CLASS, FIRE CONTROLMAN**
Korporaal Geschutmaker and
Geschutmakersmaat

**APPRENTICE FIRE CONTROLMAN,
3rd YEAR**
Leerling Geschutmaker, 3e Jaar
(Open to Seaman 1st Class only)

**APPRENTICE FIRE CONTROLMAN,
2nd YEAR**
Leerling Geschutmaker, 2e Jaar
(Open to Seaman 2nd Class only)

**APPRENTICE FIRE CONTROLMAN,
1st YEAR**
Leerling Geschutmaker, 1e Jaar
(Open to Apprentice Seaman only)

**LEADING SEAMAN AND SEAMAN
1st CLASS, ELECTRICIAN**
Korporaal Monteur and Monteursmaat

**APPRENTICE ELECTRICIAN,
3rd YEAR**
Leerling Monteur, 3e Jaar
(Open to Seaman 1st Class only)

**APPRENTICE ELECTRICIAN,
2nd YEAR**
Leerling Monteur, 2e Jaar
(Open to Seaman 2nd Class only)

**APPRENTICE ELECTRICIAN,
1st YEAR**
Leerling Monteur, 1e Jaar
(Open to Apprentice Seaman only)

**LEADING SEAMAN AND SEAMAN
1st CLASS, AVIATION REPAIRMAN**
Korporaal Vliegtuigmaker and
Vliegtuigmakersmaat

**APPRENTICE AVIATION
REPAIRMAN, 3rd YEAR**
Leerling Vliegtuigmaker, 3e Jaar
(Open to Seaman 1st Class only)

**APPRENTICE AVIATION
REPAIRMAN, 2nd YEAR**
Leerling Vliegtuigmaker, 2e Jaar
(Open to Seaman 2nd Class only)

**APPRENTICE AVIATION
REPAIRMAN, 1st YEAR**
Leerling Vliegtuigmaker, 1e Jaar
(Open to Apprentice Seaman only)

**LEADING SEAMAN, MACHINIST**
Korporaal Machinist

**LEADING SEAMAN, FIREMAN**
Korporaal Stoker

**FIREMAN-OILER**
Stoker Olieman
(Open to Seaman 1st Class only)

**FIREMAN, 1st CLASS**
Stoker 1e Klasse
(Open to Seaman 1st Class only)

**FIREMAN, 2nd CLASS**
Stoker 2e Klasse
(Open to Seaman 2nd Class only)

**LEADING SEAMAN AND SEAMAN
1st CLASS, CARPENTER**
Korporaal Timmerman and
Timmermansmaat

**APPRENTICE CARPENTER,
2nd YEAR**
Leerling Timmerman, 2e Jaar
(Open to Seaman 2nd Class only)

**APPRENTICE CARPENTER,
1st YEAR**
Leerling Timmerman, 1e Jaar
(Open to Apprentice Seaman only)

**LEADING SEAMAN AND SEAMAN
1st CLASS, STOREKEEPER**
Korporaal Bottelier and
Botteliersmaat

**LEADING SEAMAN, PILOT; SEAMAN
1st CLASS, APPRENTICE PILOT**
Korporaal Vlieger; Leerling Vlieger

**LEADING SEAMAN AND SEAMAN
1st CLASS, HOSPITAL CORPSMAN**
Korporaal Ziekenverpleger and
Ziekenverplegersmaat

**LEADING SEAMAN, MUSICIAN**
Muzikant

**ASPIRANT MUSICIAN**
Aspirant Muzikant
(Open to Seaman 1st Class only)

**APPRENTICE MUSICIAN**
Leerling Muzikant
(Open to Seaman 2nd Class only)

**SEAMAN 1st CLASS, YEOMAN;
STEWARD; COOK**
Schrijversmaat; Hofmeestersmaat;
Koksmaat

**SEAMAN 1st CLASS, BARBER;
SHOEMAKER; TAILOR**
Barbier; Schoenmaker; Kleermaker
(Under 6 years service—red; 6-12
years—yellow; over 12 years—gold)

J.A.N. No. 1:
OCTOBER 1943

# PLATE 63

**COMMISSIONED OFFICERS**

**PORTUGUESE NAVY**

**CAPTAIN, LINE**
Capitão de Mar e Guerra, Marinha

**CAP**
FOR FLAG OFFICERS

**CAP INSIGNIA**
For all Officers of the Line

**BUTTON**
All personnel

**ADMIRAL'S STAR**
Sleeves or shoulders

**SHOULDER BOARD**
Vice Admiral, Line

**LIEUTENANT COMMANDER
MEDICAL CORPS**
Capitão-Tenente, Médico

**CAP**
COMMANDER, LIEUT. COMMANDER,
AND LIEUTENANTS

**ARM INSIGNIA**

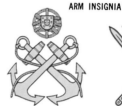

OFFICERS AT FLEET H.Q. AND
NAVAL STATIONS

**INFANTRY
INSTRUCTORS**

**COLLAR INSIGNIA**

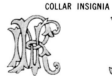

NAVAL RESERVE

RETIRED

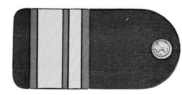

**SHOULDER BOARD**
Lieutenant Commander, Medical Corps

**ENSIGN, LINE**
Guarda-Marinha, Marinha
(Fatigue dress.  Tan or black shoes)

J.A.N. No. 1:  JUNE 1943

PLATE 64

PETTY OFFICERS

**CHIEF PETTY OFFICER, MACHINIST**
Sargento Ajudante, Condutor de Máquinas

**CAP, CHIEF BOATSWAIN'S MATE**
(Chief Petty Officers wear Commissioned
Enlisted Corps cap insignia)

**SHOULDER BOARD, CHIEF GUNNER'S MATE**

**SLEEVE INSIGNIA, CHIEF PETTY OFFICER**

**CHIEF PETTY OFFICER, MACHINIST**
Sargento Ajudante, Condutor de Máquinas

**CAP FOR PETTY OFFICERS 1st and 2nd CLASS**

**SHOULDER BOARD, GUNNER'S MATE**
**1st CLASS**

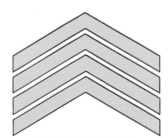

**SLEEVE INSIGNIA, PETTY OFFICER**
**1st CLASS**

**PETTY OFFICER, 1st CLASS, FIREMAN**
Primeiro Sargento Fogueiro
(Brown shoes and gloves optional with
all uniforms for Petty Officers)

**PLATE 65**

**SEAMEN**

**PORTUGUESE NAVY**

BLUE DRESS CAP

CAP BANDS FOR DRESS CAP

**N. R. P. LIMA**

SHIP'S PERSONNEL
(N.R.P. plus ship's name)

**SUBMERSÍVEIS**

SUBMARINE BASE PERSONNEL

**AVIAÇÃO**

NAVAL AIRFORCE PERSONNEL

**ARMÁDA**

SHORE PERSONNEL

**E. A. M.**

NON-RATED SEAMEN

**REFORMADO**

SEAMEN, RETIRED

LEADING SEAMAN, HOSPITAL APPRENTICE
Cabo, Aluno Enfermeiro
(White dress uniform)

SEAMAN 1st CLASS, BUGLER
Primeiro Marinheiro, Clarim
(White service uniform)

SEAMAN 2nd CLASS, TELEGRAPHIST
Segundo Marinheiro, Telegrafista
(Blue dress uniform)

APPRENTICE SEAMAN, SIGNALMAN
Grumete, Sinaleiro
(Fatigue uniform)

PLATE 66

**COMMISSIONED OFFICERS**

**RUSSIAN NAVY**

All items illustrated below (except star in cap insignia and visor for Captain 1st Rank through Captain 3rd Rank) show gold or silver in accordance with color of braid on shoulder board. Corps Officers (except Line-Engineering) use Army titles.

**CAP INSIGNIA**
All Commissioned and Warrant Officers

**CAP VISORS**

Flag and General Officers

Captain 1st Rank through Captain 3rd Rank, Line and Line-Engineering. Plain visor for lower ranks and for all other Corps Officers below Major General.

BUTTON
Worn by Flag and General Officers on wide shoulder boards.

MARINES' INSIGNIA
Worn on Navy uniform; upper left sleeve.

BUTTON
Coat button, all ranks. On General Officer's narrow shoulder boards; on all wide boards below Flag or General Officer rank.

**REAR ADMIRAL, LINE**
Kontr-admiral
(Standard service uniform)

**CAPTAIN 3rd RANK, LINE**
Kapitan tret'yevo ranga
(Summer service uniform. White trousers, white shoes optional)

**CAPTAIN LIEUTENANT, LINE**
Kapitan-leytenant
(Semi-dress uniform. Same uniform in white, with sleeve stripes and shoulder boards, for Flag Officers only)

**SENIOR LIEUTENANT, LINE**
Starshiy leytenant
(Winter Overcoat)

J.A.N. No. 1, February, 1945   DIVISION OF NAVAL INTELLIGENCE

# PLATE 67

## SHOULDER BOARDS AND SLEEVE INSIGNIA; LINE OFFICERS  ## SHOULDER BOARDS; CORPS OFFICERS  ## RUSSIAN NAVY

SHOULDER BOARDS: Worn by all Commissioned Officers, on all uniform jackets and overcoats. Corps shoulder boards differ from Line as illustrated at far right.

SLEEVE STRIPES: Restricted to Line and Line-Engineering Officers. Worn on all jackets except high collar white. Not worn on overcoat.

Corps shoulder boards have same number of rank stripes and stars as Line. Line-Engineering uses Navy (Line) titles; other Corps, Army titles. Corps Officers (except Line-Engineering) are further distinguished by absence of usual rank stripes on sleeves.

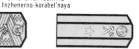

**LINE-ENGINEERING**
Inzhenerno-korabel'naya

Rear Admiral — Captain, 3rd Rank

| ADMIRAL OF THE FLEET Admiral flota | ADMIRAL Admiral | VICE ADMIRAL Vitse-admiral |
|---|---|---|

**COASTAL DEFENSE** Beregovaya — Major General / Major

**NAVAL AVIATION** Aviatsiya — Major General / Major

| REAR ADMIRAL Kontr-admiral | CAPTAIN, 1st RANK Kapitan pervovo ranga | CAPTAIN, 2nd RANK Kapitan vtorovo ranga | CAPTAIN, 3rd RANK Kapitan tret'yevo ranga |
|---|---|---|---|

**NAVAL CONSTRUCTION** Inzhenerno-beregovaya — Major General / Major

**AVIATION ENGINEERING** Inzhenerno-aviatsionnaya — Major General / Major

**SUPPLY** Intendantskaya — Major General / Major

**MEDICAL (MILITARY MEDICAL TRAINING)** Meditsinskaya (Voyenno-meditsinskim obrazovaniyem) — Major General / Major

| CAPTAIN LIEUTENANT Kapitan-leytenant | SENIOR LIEUTENANT Starshiy leytenant | LIEUTENANT Leytenant | JUNIOR LIEUTENANT Mladshiy leytenant |
|---|---|---|---|

**MEDICAL (WITHOUT MILITARY MEDICAL TRAINING)** Meditsinskaya (Bez voyenno-meditsinskovo obrazovaniya) — Major General / Major

**VETERINARY** Veterinarnaya — Major General / Major

**LEGAL** Yustitsiya — Major General / Major

**ADMINISTRATION** Administrativnaya (Limited to Colonel and below) — Major

### CORPS SLEEVE INSIGNIA

Corps Officers (except Line-Engineering) have Army titles and no sleeve stripes; with full dress, insignia as shown here is worn on cuffs. Braid and piping are always same color as on shoulder board.

| GENERAL OFFICERS, AVIATION ENGINEERING | COLONEL THROUGH MAJOR, COASTAL DEFENSE | CAPTAIN THROUGH JUNIOR LIEUTENANT, NAVAL CONSTRUCTION |
|---|---|---|

### CORPS SHOULDER EMBLEMS

Corps shoulder boards are distinguished by differences in color of braid, stars and piping, and in some instances by the addition of the emblems shown at right.

**LINE-ENGINEERING** (below Flag rank: silver); NAVAL CONSTRUCTION; AVIATION ENGINEERING

**MEDICAL; VETERINARY** (silver)

**LEGAL**

J.A.N. No. 1
February, 1945
DIVISION OF NAVAL
INTELLIGENCE

PLATE 68

WARRANT OFFICERS, PETTY OFFICERS AND SEAMEN

**WORKING CAP FOR AVIATION AND SUBMARINE SERVICE**
Officers and Men

**CAP INSIGNIA, PETTY OFFICER 1st CLASS AND BELOW**

**CAP INSIGNIA, CHIEF PETTY OFFICER**
(Worn on cap with visor. Warrant Officer wears Commissioned Officer's cap insignia)

КРАСНЫЙ КАВКАЗ

**UNIT CITATION CAP BAND**
(With ship's name)
PO 1st Class and below.

**WARRANT OFFICER, SIGNALMAN**
Michman, Signal'shchik
(Standard service uniform. Extra-service chevron. Same uniform also for CPO)

I.A.N. No. 1, February, 1945   DIVISION OF NAVAL INTELLIGENCE

**PETTY OFFICER 1st CLASS, FIRE CONTROLMAN**
Starshina pervoy stat'i, Dal'nomershchik
(Standard service uniform. Name of ship or fleet on cap band)

**PETTY OFFICER 2nd CLASS, TELEGRAPHIST**
Starshina vtoroy stat'i, Telegrafist
(Standard working uniform. Cap with visor for 5 years' service)

**SEAMAN**
Krasnoflotets
(Summer service uniform. Baltic Fleet)

**PLATE 69**

## WARRANT OFFICERS, PETTY OFFICERS AND SEAMEN

**SHOULDER BOARDS**—Worn by Warrant Officer and CPO on jackets and by all ratings on long and short overcoats.

| WARRANT OFFICER | CHIEF PETTY OFFICER | PETTY OFFICER, 1st CLASS | PETTY OFFICER, 2nd CLASS | LEADING SEAMAN | SEAMAN | JUNIOR APPRENTICE |
|---|---|---|---|---|---|---|
| Michman | Glavnyy starshina | Starshina pervoy stat'i (Black Sea Fleet) | Starshina vtoroy stat'i (Black Sea Fleet) | Starshiy krasnoflotets (Black Sea Fleet) | Krasnoflotets (Black Sea Fleet) | Yunga |

MIDSHIPMEN wear jumper-type uniform and any of the shoulder boards illustrated above and at right (except that of Junior Apprentice). They are distinguished by an anchor pinned to the shoulder board: gold for Line and Line-Engineering; silver, with silver braid, for Medical and Supply.

**SHOULDER BOARDS**—For jumpers only.

| PETTY OFFICER, 1st CLASS | PETTY OFFICER, 2nd CLASS | LEADING SEAMAN | SEAMAN (Black Sea Fleet) | JUNIOR APPRENTICE |
|---|---|---|---|---|

**UNIT DESIGNATIONS**—Worn on large shoulder boards by PO 1st Class through Seaman; on small shoulder boards by Seaman.

| | | | |
|---|---|---|---|
| ТФ | PACIFIC FLEET | ВФ | VOLGA RIVER FLOTILLA |
| БФ | BALTIC FLEET | ОФ | LAKE ONEGA FLOTILLA |
| ЧФ | BLACK SEA FLEET | Ф | UNASSIGNED; also, CPO |
| СФ | ARCTIC FLEET | | |
| АФ | AMUR RIVER FLOTILLA | ИТ | ADVANCED ENGINEERING SCHOOL |
| КФ | CASPIAN SEA FLOTILLA | БО | COAST ARTILLERY SCHOOL |

| | |
|---|---|
| ПО | ANTI-AIRCRAFT SCHOOL |
| С | STALIN NAVAL AVIATION SCHOOL |
| Л | LEVANEVSKI NAVAL AVIATION SCHOOL |
| М | MOLOTOFF AVIATION ENGINEERING SCHOOL |
| ПУ | NAVAL POLITICAL INSTITUTE |
| Ю | JUNIOR APPRENTICE |

PETTY OFFICER, 1st CLASS
Starshina pervoy stat'i
(Long overcoat, Pacific Fleet)

LEADING SEAMAN
Starshiy krasnoflotets
(Short overcoat, Black Sea Fleet)

J.A.N. No. 1, February, 1945  DIVISION OF NAVAL INTELLIGENCE

PLATE 70

# WARRANT OFFICERS, PETTY OFFICERS AND SEAMEN

RUSSIAN NAVY

## SPECIALTY INSIGNIA

Specialty Insignia appear on the upper left sleeve of jumpers, jackets and overcoats for all grades; with Warrant Officer and Chief Petty Officer the surrounding circle is gold, the inner figure remaining red; all lower grades are red throughout, as illustrated.

**MARINES' INSIGNIA**
Worn on Navy uniform;
upper left sleeve.

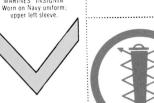

**EXTRA-SERVICE CHEVRON**
Upper left sleeve
(One chevron—over five years;
two chevrons—over ten years;
three chevrons—over fifteen years)

**WOUND STRIPES**
Upper right sleeve

Major wound

Minor wound

**BUTTON**

**BELT BUCKLE**

J A N No. 1
February, 1945
DIVISION OF NAVAL
INTELLIGENCE

QUARTERMASTER
Rulevoy

GYRO COMPASS TECHNICIAN
Elektrik shturmanskiy

FIRE CONTROLMAN
Dal'nomershchik

GUNNER
Komendor

ORDNANCE ELECTRICIAN
Elektrik artilleriyskiy

METEOROLOGIST
Spetsialist meteosluzhby

MINE MAN
Miner

TORPEDOMAN
Torpedist

ELECTRICIAN-TORPEDOMAN
Elektrik torpednyy

RADIOMAN
Radist

TELEGRAPHIST
Telegrafist

SIGNALMAN
Signal'shchik

RADIO TECHNICIAN
Radioelektrik

DIVER
Vodolaz

MACHINIST-BOILERMAKER
Mashinist kotel'noy

WATER TENDER
Mashinist tryumnoy

MACHINIST
Mashinist

MOTORMAN
Motorist

ELECTRICIAN
Elektrik

CHEMIST
Khimist

BOATSWAIN
Botsman

RIGGER
Marsovoy

MUSICIAN
Muzykant

STOREKEEPER
Kladovshchik

HOSPITAL CORPSMAN
Sanitar

# PLATE 71

## COMMISSIONED OFFICERS

CAP FOR CAPTAINS, COMMANDERS
AND LIEUTENANT COMMANDERS
OF THE LINE

CAP INSIGNIA, LINE OFFICERS

BUTTON

SHOULDER BOARD
LIEUTENANT COMMANDER,
ENGINEERING CORPS

**COMMANDER, LINE**
Capitan de Fragata, Cuerpo General
(White or Blue Hat)

The regulation stripes for all officers is from seam to seam on the outer face of the blue uniform sleeves. However, many officers still wear the shorter, 3½ inch stripes required prior to 1941.

**LIEUTENANT COMMANDER
ENGINEERING CORPS**
Comandante, Cuerpo Maquinista

CORPS INSIGNIA AND CORPS COLORS

 ENGINEERING Maquinistas

 ORDNANCE Artilleria

 SUPPLY Intendencia

 MEDICAL Sanidad

NAVAL CONSTRUCTION Ingenieros Navales

LEGAL Juridico

 MARINES Infanteria de Marina

The colors used to designate the different Corps appear as a background for the sleeve stripes, for the shoulder board stripes, and for the anchor in the hat device. The Corps Insignia appear only on the sleeves and shoulder boards, replacing the loop which signifies Line.

**LIEUTENANT, ORDNANCE CORPS**
Capitan, Cuerpo Artilleria
(Fatigue uniform; white or blue hat)

J.A.N. No. 1  MARCH 1943

PLATE 72

# WARRANT OFFICER, CHIEF AND FIRST CLASS PETTY OFFICER

SPANISH NAVY

**CAP**
For Junior Commissioned and Warrant Officer

**CAP INSIGNIA**
For Commissioned and Warrant Officer

BUTTON

**TORPEDOMAN (Warrant Officer)**
Contramaestre Mayor, Torpedista
Submarine Service

**CAP**
For Chief and First Class Petty Officer

**SHOULDER BOARD (Boatswain)**
For Warrant Officer, Chief and
First Class Petty Officer

**CHIEF BOATSWAIN'S MATE (Chief Petty Officer)**
Contramaestre Primero, Contramaestre

**MACHINIST'S MATE, FIRST CLASS**
(Petty Officer, First Class)
Contramaestre Segundo, Mecânico Fatigue Dress

J A N No. 1   MARCH 1943

## PLATE 73

**PETTY OFFICERS, 2nd AND 3rd CLASS, AND SEAMEN**

STEEL HELMET WORN BY ALL PERSONNEL
IN COMBAT AREA

RATING INSIGNIA

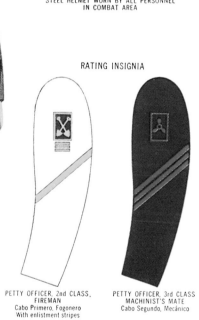

PETTY OFFICER, 2nd CLASS,
FIREMAN
Cabo Primero, Fogonero
With enlistment stripes

PETTY OFFICER, 3rd CLASS
MACHINIST'S MATE
Cabo Segundo, Mecánico

**PETTY OFFICER, 2nd CLASS**
Cabo Primero
Fatigue and landing dress

CAP

RATING INSIGNIA

SEAMAN, TORPEDOMAN
Marinero, torpedista

APPRENTICE SEAMAN,
HYDROGRAPHER
Ayudante, hidrógrafo

**SEAMAN ARTIFICER**
Marinero de Oficio

**GUNNER'S MATE, 3rd CLASS**
Cabo Segundo, Artillero

## PLATE 74

## COAST ARTILLERY; OFFICERS AND MEN

**SWEDISH NAVY**

THE COAST ARTILLERY (Kustartilleriet) is concerned with coastal defense, including the mining of coastal areas and adjacent waters. Although their titles and uniforms are similar to those of the Army, the Coast Artillery is a branch of the Navy.

CORPS COLORS—Bronze for Line, lilac for Chaplains, orange for Special Service. Worn by all personnel as piping around collar insignia; by General through Warrant Officer also as a collar piping. See examples immediately below at left.

Special Service, which includes all personnel except Line and Chaplains, has orange diamonds instead of stars.

**CAP INSIGNIA**
Commissioned Officers

**SHOULDER BOARD EMBLEM**
All personnel

**COLLAR INSIGNIA; LINE AND CORPS** Showing piping and position of insignia     **SHOULDER BOARDS; ALL PERSONNEL** Only General Officers show specific rank

**MAJOR, LINE**
Major

**CHAPLAIN**
Militärpastor
(Commissioned but without specific rank)

**MAJOR,**
**SPECIAL SERVICE**
Major, Civilmilitär

**MAJOR GENERAL**
General, three stars,
Lt. Gen., two

**COLONEL; LT. COL;**
**AND MAJOR**

**CAPTAIN THROUGH**
**PRIVATE**

### COLLAR INSIGNIA; LINE
Since all General Officers wear same collar insignia, their individual rank is shown by stars on shoulder boards. Numerals on insignia of Sergeant and below are regiment numbers.

**GENERAL; LT. GEN;**
**MAJ. GEN.**
General; Generallöjtnant;
Generalmajor

**COLONEL**
Överste

**LIEUTENANT COLONEL**
Överstelöjtnant

**MAJOR**
Major

**CAPTAIN**
Kapten

**1st LIEUT; CHIEF**
**WARRANT OFFICER**
Löjtnant; Förvaltningsunderofficer
or Regementskassör av 1 klassen

**2nd LIEUT;**
**WARRANT OFFICER**
Fänrik; Flaggunderofficer or
Regementskassör av 2 klassen

**SERGEANT MAJOR**
Underofficer av 2 graden

**SERGEANT**
Furir

**CORPORAL**
Korpral

**PRIVATE, 1st CLASS**
Vicekorpral

**PRIVATE**
Menig

**MAJOR, LINE**
Major

**CORPORAL, HOSPITAL CORPSMAN**
Korpral, Sjukvårdare

J.A.N. No. 1.
JUNE 1945
Division of
Naval
Intelligence

PLATE 75

**OFFICERS AND MEN**

**LIEUTENANT (jg), LINE**
Löjtnant
(Blue service uniform.
White cap cover permitted)

**CAP FOR ADMIRAL,
VICE ADMIRAL AND REAR ADMIRAL**
Plain visor for all other officers

**INSIGNIA FOR WINTER CAP;
COMMISSIONED OFFICERS**

**OVERSEAS CAP; SEAMEN ONLY**
For shipboard use.

**CAP INSIGNIA;
PETTY OFFICER RESTRICTED-IN-GRADE**
Worn on cap with visor.

**CAP INSIGNIA; COMMISSIONED OFFICERS**

**WINTER CAP**
Illustrated for Commissioned Officer.
Chief Warrant, Warrant and CPO.
use insignia shown at right.

**GOTLAND**

**SEAMAN'S CAP BAND**
(With ship's name)
For ship's personnel.

**BUTTON; ALL PERSONNEL**

**CAP FOR CHIEF WARRANT,
WARRANT AND CHIEF PETTY OFFICER**

**CAP INSIGNIA, CHIEF WARRANT, WARRANT
AND CHIEF PETTY OFFICER**
Silver anchor for Drafted Personnel.

**KUNGL. FLOTTAN**

**SEAMAN'S CAP**
Cap band for shore personnel.
(Translation: "Royal Navy")

**CAP INSIGNIA; PETTY OFFICER (NOT CPO)**
Worn on cap with visor.

**SEAMAN 1st CLASS, GUNNER**
Korpral, Artillerimatros
(Blue dress uniform.
White cap cover permitted)

J.A.N. No. 1
JUNE 1945
Division of
Naval
Intelligence

PLATE 76

**COMMISSIONED OFFICERS**

**TURKISH NAVY**

CAP FOR NON-COMBAT CAPTAINS,
COMMANDERS, LIEUTENANT COMMANDERS

CAP INSIGNIA, COMBAT OFFICERS, LINE

**COMMODORE, STAFF CORPS**
Kurmay Tuğamiral
(White trousers permitted)

**COMMANDER, SUPPLY CORPS**
Levazim Yarbay
(Army uniform; for Navy Officers
serving ashore in fortified areas)

BUTTON

**SUBMARINE SERVICE**
Worn low on left breast

**LIEUTENANT, ENGINEERING CORPS**
Makine Üsteğmen
(Fatigue Uniform)

**ENSIGN, LINE**
Güverte Asteğmen

J.A.N. No. 1: AUGUST 1943

# PLATE 77

**PETTY OFFICERS AND SEAMEN**

SHOULDER BOARD,
CHIEF PETTY OFFICER, SIGNALMAN

CAP INSIGNIA, CHIEF PETTY OFFICER
(Corps color appears as background
for anchor)

CAP INSIGNIA, PROFESSIONAL
PERSONNEL BELOW C.P.O.
(Corps color appears as background)

SUBMARINE SERVICE
(Drafted personnel)

**CHIEF PETTY OFFICER, BOATSWAIN**
Porsun Başgedikli
(Professional)

**CHIEF PETTY OFFICER, SIGNALMAN**
Sancak Başgedikli
(Professional)

**PETTY OFFICER, 1st CLASS,
TORPEDOMAN**
Torpitocu Gedikli Başçavuş
(Professional. Submarine Service)

**LEADING SEAMAN, MACHINIST**
Motorcu Cavuş
(Drafted)

J.A.N. No. 1: AUGUST 1943

PLATE 78

The National Geographic Magazine

Rear Admiral

Commander

Lieutenant
Junior Grade

Warrant Officer
(Carpenter)

Vice Admiral

Captain

Lieutenant

Chief Warrant Officer
(Boatswain)

Admiral

Commodore

Lieutenant
Commander

Ensign

Aviation
Cadet

NAVY SHOULDER MARKS AND SLEEVE STRIPES

Garrison Cap
(Lieutenant)

Aviator's Garrison Cap

Embroidered Cap Device

Captain and Commander
(Summer)

Bandsman
(Full Dress)

Nurse

Flag Rank

Warrant Officer

Nurse's Hat Device

Lieutenant Commander
and Lower Ranks
(Summer-Working)

Metal Cap Device

NAVY CAPS AND CAP DEVICES

PLATE 79

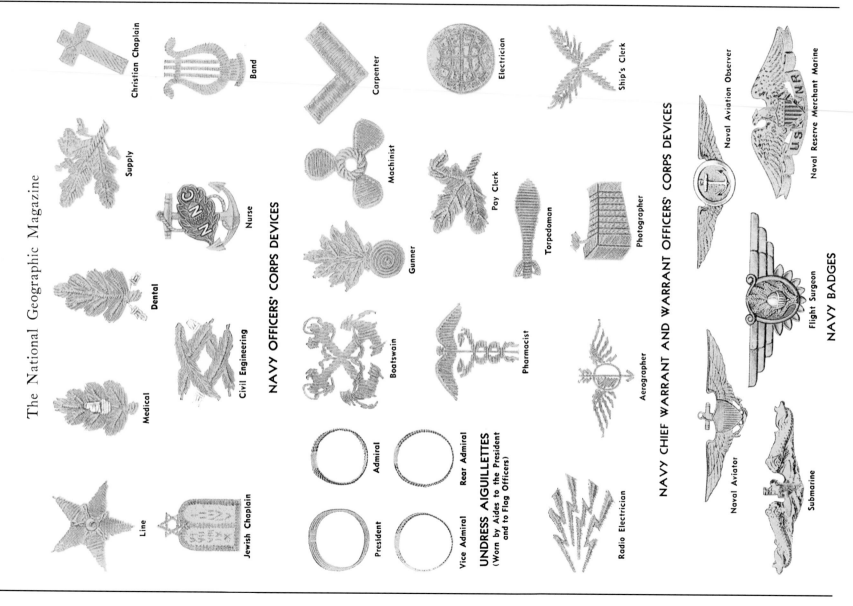

The National Geographic Magazine

Christian Chaplain

Band

Carpenter

Electrician

Ship's Clerk

Naval Aviation Observer

Naval Reserve Merchant Marine

Supply

Nurse

Machinist

Pay Clerk

Torpedoman

Photographer

Dental

Gunner

NAVY OFFICERS' CORPS DEVICES

Civil Engineering

Medical

Boatswain

Pharmacist

Aerographer

Flight Surgeon

NAVY CHIEF WARRANT AND WARRANT OFFICERS' CORPS DEVICES

NAVY BADGES

Line

Jewish Chaplain

Admiral

Rear Admiral

President

Vice Admiral

UNDRESS AIGUILLETTES
(Worn by Aides to the President
and to Flag Officers)

Radio Electrician

Naval Aviator

Submarine

PLATE 80

The National Geographic Magazine

Captain

Rear Admiral

Vice Admiral

Admiral

Ensign

Lieutenant Junior Grade

Lieutenant

Lieutenant Commander

Commander

## NAVY PIN-ON MINIATURE RANK DEVICES

Civil Engineering

Jewish Chaplain

Christian Chaplain

Supply

Dental

Medical

## NAVY OFFICERS' PIN-ON MINIATURE CORPS DEVICES

Carpenter

Radio Electrician

Machinist

Electrician

Gunner

Pay Clerk

Boatswain

Pharmacist

## NAVY CHIEF WARRANT OFFICERS' PIN-ON MINIATURE CORPS DEVICES
(Warrant Officers—Same Devices in Gold)

SP
Shore Patrol

Geneva Cross

17
Sick-List Badge

## NAVY BRASSARDS

Lt., Asst. Supt. Navy Nurse Corps

Ensign, Nurse

Lt. Comdr., Asst. Supt. Navy Nurse Corps

Lt. (jg), Chief Nurse

## NURSES' WHITE UNIFORM CAPS

Officers' Cook and Steward

Blue Cap

Chief Petty Officer (Summer)

White Hat

## NAVY ENLISTED MEN'S CAPS

PLATE 81

The National Geographic Magazine

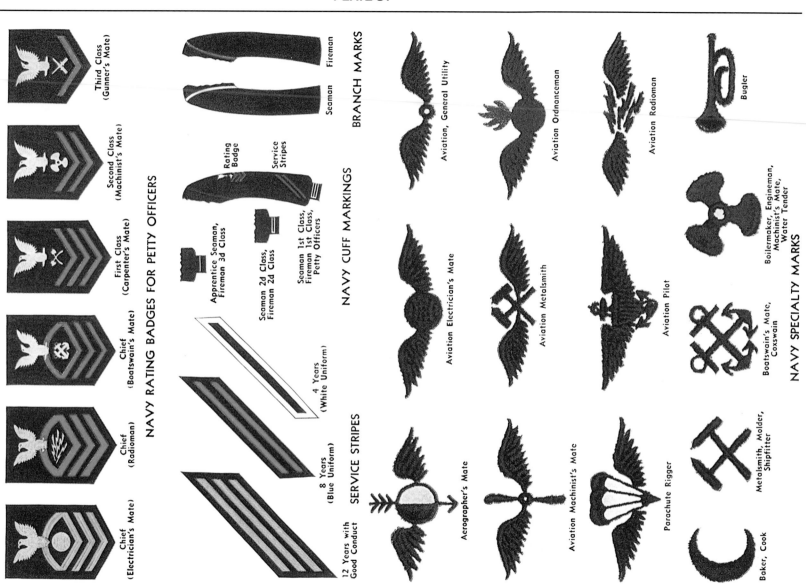

NAVY RATING BADGES FOR PETTY OFFICERS

Third Class (Gunner's Mate)

Second Class (Machinist's Mate)

First Class (Carpenter's Mate)

Chief (Boatswain's Mate)

Chief (Radioman)

Chief (Electrician's Mate)

Fireman

Seaman

Rating Badge

Service Stripes

Apprentice Seaman, Fireman 3d Class

Seaman 2d Class, Fireman 2d Class

Seaman 1st Class, Fireman 1st Class, Petty Officers

BRANCH MARKS

NAVY CUFF MARKINGS

4 Years (White Uniform)

8 Years (Blue Uniform)

12 Years with Good Conduct

SERVICE STRIPES

Aviation, General Utility

Aviation Ordnanceman

Aviation Radioman

Bugler

Aviation Electrician's Mate

Aviation Metalsmith

Aviation Pilot

Boilermaker, Engineman, Machinist's Mate, Water Tender

Aerographer's Mate

Aviation Machinist's Mate

Parachute Rigger

Boatswain's Mate, Coxswain

NAVY SPECIALTY MARKS

Metalsmith, Molder, Shipfitter

Baker, Cook

PLATE 82

The National Geographic Magazine

Gunner's Mate

Photographer's Mate

Radioman, Radio Technician, Telegrapher

Officers' Steward, 1st Class; Officers' Cook, 1st Class (Size Reduced)

Fire Controlman

Musician

Radarman

Storekeeper

Yeoman

Electrician's Mate

Chief Commissary Steward

Motor Machinist's Mate

Quartermaster

Soundman

Turret Captain

Carpenter's Mate, Painter, Pattern Maker

Hospital Apprentice, Pharmacist's Mate

Printer

Signalman

Torpedoman's Mate

**NAVY SPECIALTY MARKS**

Photographer

Welfare

Inspector of Naval Material

Transport Airman

Mail Clerk

Teacher

I.B.M. Operator

Shore Patrol

Gunnery Instructor

Athletic Instructor

Recruiter

**NAVY SPECIALIST RATINGS**

PLATE 83

The National Geographic Magazine

Gun Pointer First Class (Size Reduced)

Radioman

Master Horizontal Bomber (Size Reduced)

Airship Insignia

Officers' Cook and Steward

(30-line, Blue Uniform)

(30-line—White Uniform)

Gun Pointer Second Class

Construction Battalion

Diver, First Class

Enlisted Man (30-line—Dungaree)

Enlisted Man (25-line—Trouser)

Mine Warfare

Signalman

Parachute Man

NAVY DISTINGUISHING MARKS

Gun Captain

Bombsight Mechanic

Expert Rifleman, Expert Pistol Shot

Navy "E" in Gunnery

Navy "E" in Engineering

Ex-Apprentice

Master Diver

Enlisted Man (50-line—Overcoat)

NAVY BUTTONS

Seaman Gunner

Gun Range Finder Operator

Rifle Sharpshooter

Aerial Gunner

Submarine Insignia

Officer (40-line—Overcoat)

Officer (35-line—Service Coat)

PLATE 84

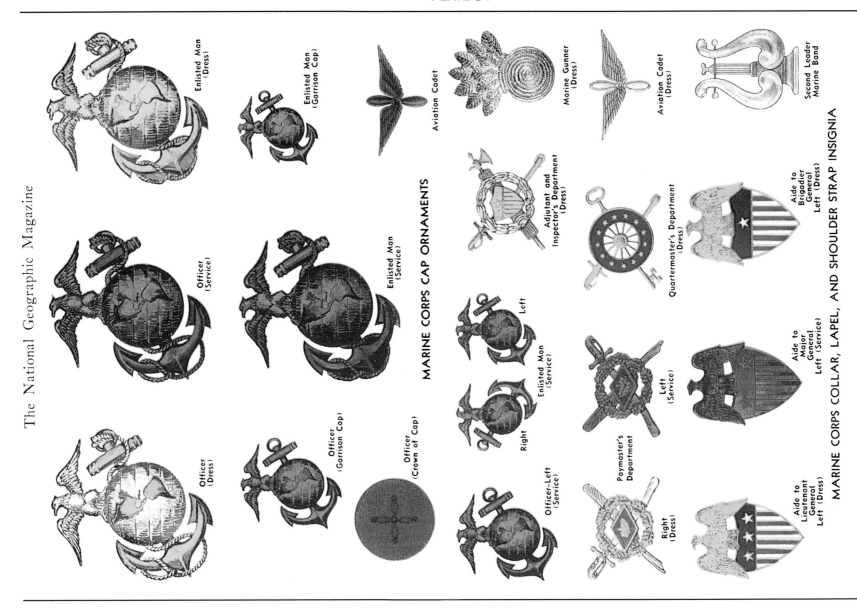

The National Geographic Magazine

Enlisted Man (Dress)

Enlisted Man (Garrison Cap)

Aviation Cadet

Marine Gunner (Dress)

Aviation Cadet (Dress)

Second Leader Marine Band

Officer (Service)

Enlisted Man (Service)

Adjutant and Inspector's Department (Dress)

Quartermaster's Department (Dress)

Aide to Brigadier General Left (Dress)

Officer (Dress)

Officer (Garrison Cap)

Officer (Crown of Cap)

Left

Enlisted Man (Service)

Right

Officer-Left (Service)

Paymaster's Department

Left (Service)

Right (Dress)

Aide to Major General Left (Service)

Aide to Lieutenant General Left (Dress)

**MARINE CORPS CAP ORNAMENTS**

**MARINE CORPS COLLAR, LAPEL, AND SHOULDER STRAP INSIGNIA**

PLATE 85

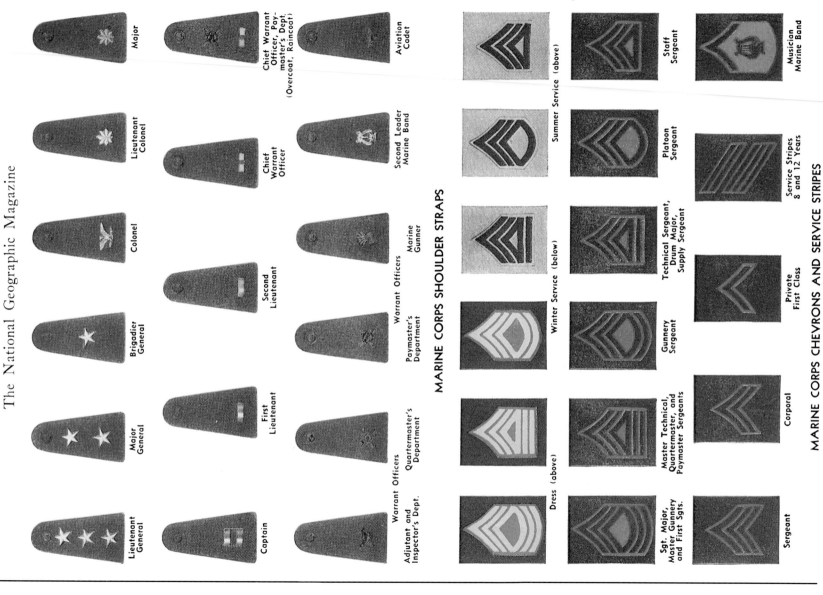

The National Geographic Magazine

Major

Lieutenant Colonel

Colonel

Brigadier General

Major General

Lieutenant General

Chief Warrant Officer, Pay-master's Dept. (Overcoat, Raincoat)

Chief Warrant Officer

Second Lieutenant

Warrant Officers Paymaster's Department

Warrant Officers Quartermaster's Department

First Lieutenant

Captain

Warrant Officers Adjutant and Inspector's Dept.

Aviation Cadet

Second Leader Marine Band

Marine Gunner

**MARINE CORPS SHOULDER STRAPS**

Summer Service (above)

Winter Service (below)

Dress (above)

Staff Sergeant

Platoon Sergeant

Technical Sergeant, Drum Major, Supply Sergeant

Gunnery Sergeant

Master Technical, Quartermaster, and Paymaster Sergeants

Sgt. Major, Master Gunnery and First Sgts.

Musician Marine Band

Service Stripes 8 and 12 Years

Private First Class

Corporal

Sergeant

**MARINE CORPS CHEVRONS AND SERVICE STRIPES**

PLATE 86

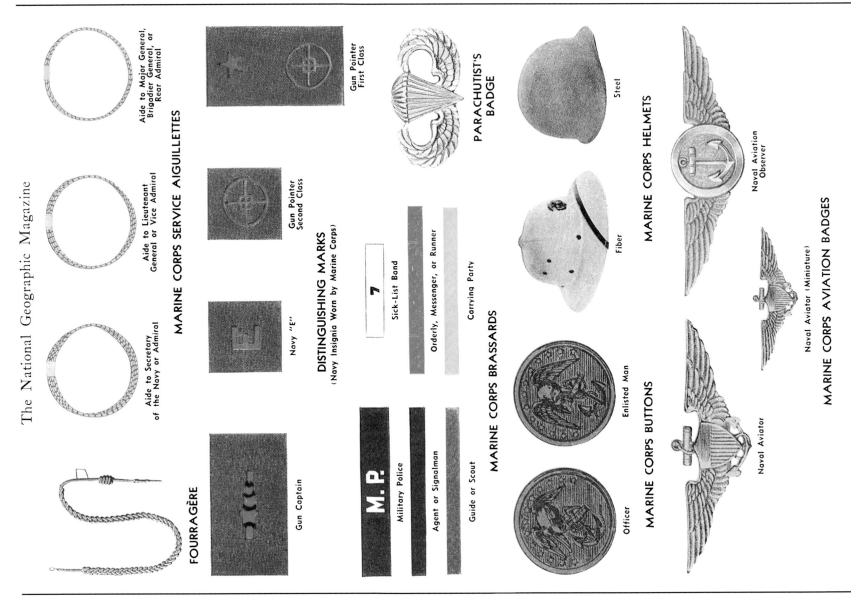

The National Geographic Magazine

FOURRAGÈRE

MARINE CORPS SERVICE AIGUILLETTES

Aide to Major General,
Brigadier General, or
Rear Admiral

Aide to Lieutenant
General or Vice Admiral

Aide to Secretary
of the Navy or Admiral

Gun Captain

DISTINGUISHING MARKS
(Navy Insignia Worn by Marine Corps)

Gun Pointer
First Class

Gun Pointer
Second Class

Navy "E"

MARINE CORPS BRASSARDS

Sick-List Band

Orderly, Messenger, or Runner

Carrying Party

Military Police

Agent or Signalman

Guide or Scout

MARINE CORPS BUTTONS

Enlisted Man

Officer

PARACHUTIST'S
BADGE

MARINE CORPS HELMETS

Steel

Fiber

MARINE CORPS AVIATION BADGES

Naval Aviation
Observer

Naval Aviator (Miniature)

Naval Aviator

# PLATE 87

The National Geographic Magazine

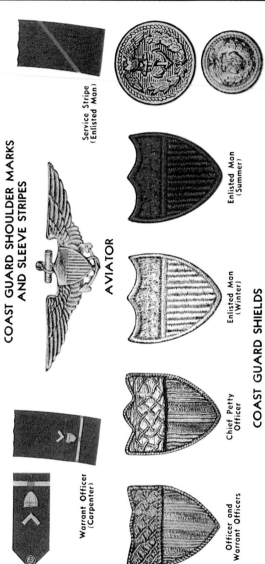

Captain

Lieutenant

Chief Warrant Officer
(Carpenter)

Rear Admiral

Lieutenant
Commander

Ensign

Vice Admiral

Commander

Lieutenant
Junior Grade

Warrant Officer
(Carpenter)

COAST GUARD SHOULDER MARKS
AND SLEEVE STRIPES

Service Stripe
(Enlisted Man)

AVIATOR

Enlisted Man
(Summer)

Enlisted Man
(Winter)

Chief Petty
Officer

Officer and
Warrant Officers

COAST GUARD SHIELDS

BUTTONS

U.S.C.G.

Shore Establishments

Officers' Steward

Chief Petty
Officer

Warrant Officer

Officer and Chief Warrant Officer

COAST GUARD CAP INSIGNIA

**PLATE 88**

The National Geographic Magazine

Petty Officer
Second Class
(Quartermaster)

Chief Petty
Officer
(Boatswain's Mate)

Petty Officer
Third Class
(Electrician's Mate)

Petty Officer
First Class
(Gunner's Mate)

**COAST GUARD
RATING BADGES**

Electrician

Machinist

Ship's Clerk

Pharmacist

Pay Clerk

Photographer

Gunner

Boatswain

Carpenter

Radio Electrician

**COAST GUARD CHIEF WARRANT OFFICERS
AND WARRANT OFFICERS' SPECIALTY DEVICES**

Aviation Pilot

Aviation Metalsmith

Aviation Machinist's Mate

Bugler

Boatswain's Mate,
Coxswain

Gunner's Mate

Cook, Baker

Chief Commissary
Steward

Carpenter's Mate,
Painter, Pattern
Maker

Musician

Machinist's Mate,
Boilermaker, Engineman,
Water Tender

Quartermaster

Electrician's Mate

Printer

Yeoman

Photographer's Mate

Storekeeper

Pharmacist's Mate,
Hospital Apprentice

Signalman

Radioman, Radio
Technician,
Telegrapher

**COAST GUARD SPECIALTY MARKS**

PLATE 89

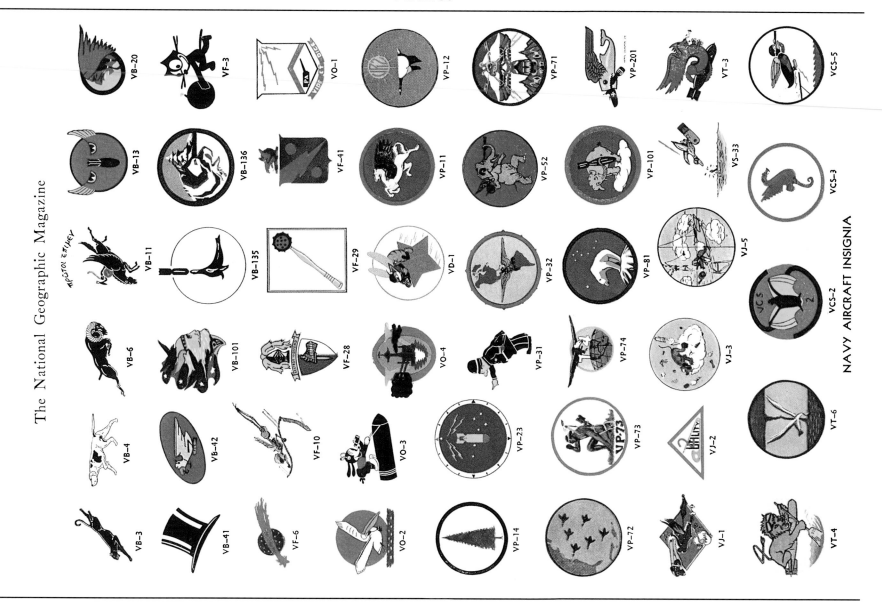

The National Geographic Magazine

NAVY AIRCRAFT INSIGNIA

PLATE 90

The National Geographic Magazine

Ranger

TTS–Atlantic

Pearl Harbor

MAW–1

VMSB–131

ZMQ–1

VF–71

VT–5

Enterprise

TTS–Pacific

Norman

Seattle

VMF–211

VMJ–252

VF–5

VT–2

VCS–9

CQTU–G.L.

Jacksonville

San Diego

VMF–111

VMS–3

VF–2

VS–72

VCS–8

CASU–3

Hutchinson

VB–5

VS–71

VCS–7

Wright

Coco Solo

Quonset

MAG–21

VMSB–232

Yorktown

VS–5

VCS–6

Saratoga

Cape May

Pensacola

MAW–11

VMSB–231

Lexington

Langley

VF–72

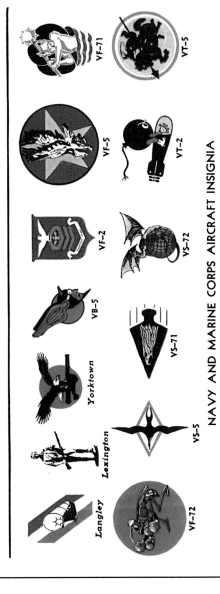

NAVY AND MARINE CORPS AIRCRAFT INSIGNIA

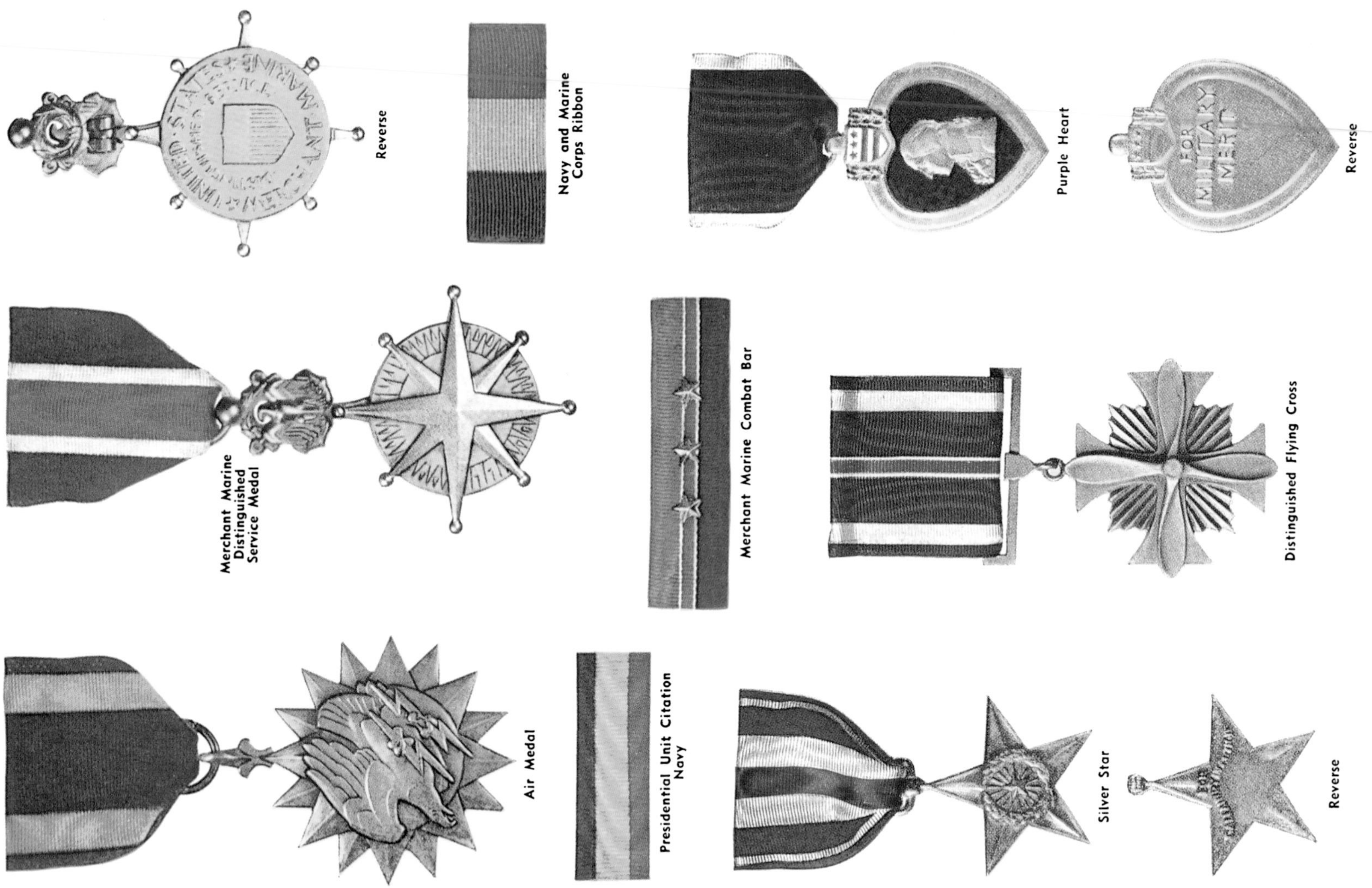

PLATE 91

Reverse

Navy and Marine Corps Ribbon

Purple Heart

Reverse

FOR MILITARY MERIT

Merchant Marine Distinguished Service Medal

Merchant Marine Combat Bar

Distinguished Flying Cross

Air Medal

Presidential Unit Citation Navy

Silver Star

Reverse

DECORATIONS, MEDALS, AND RIBBONS AUTHORIZED DURING WORLD WAR II

PLATE 92

Distinguished
Service Medal

Reverse

Specially Meritorious
Medal

Medal of Honor
(Authorized 1861)

Medal of Honor
(Obsolete)

Gold Star

Reverse

Navy Cross

Reverse

Brevet Medal (Marine Corps)

The National Geographic Magazine

NAVY AND MARINE CORPS DECORATIONS

PLATE 93

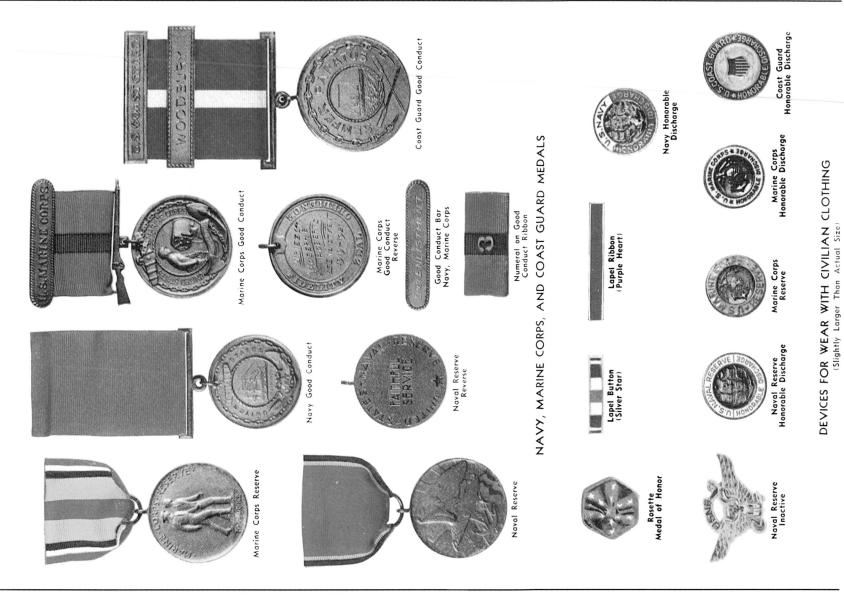

Coast Guard Good Conduct

Marine Corps Good Conduct

Marine Corps Good Conduct Reverse

Good Conduct Bar Navy, Marine Corps

Numeral on Good Conduct Ribbon

Navy Good Conduct

Naval Reserve Reverse

Marine Corps Reserve

Naval Reserve

Navy Honorable Discharge

Coast Guard Honorable Discharge

Marine Corps Honorable Discharge

Marine Corps Reserve

Naval Reserve Honorable Discharge

Lapel Ribbon (Purple Heart)

Lapel Button (Silver Star)

Rosette Medal of Honor

Naval Reserve Inactive

## NAVY, MARINE CORPS, AND COAST GUARD MEDALS

## DEVICES FOR WEAR WITH CIVILIAN CLOTHING
(Slightly Larger Than Actual Size)

PLATE 94

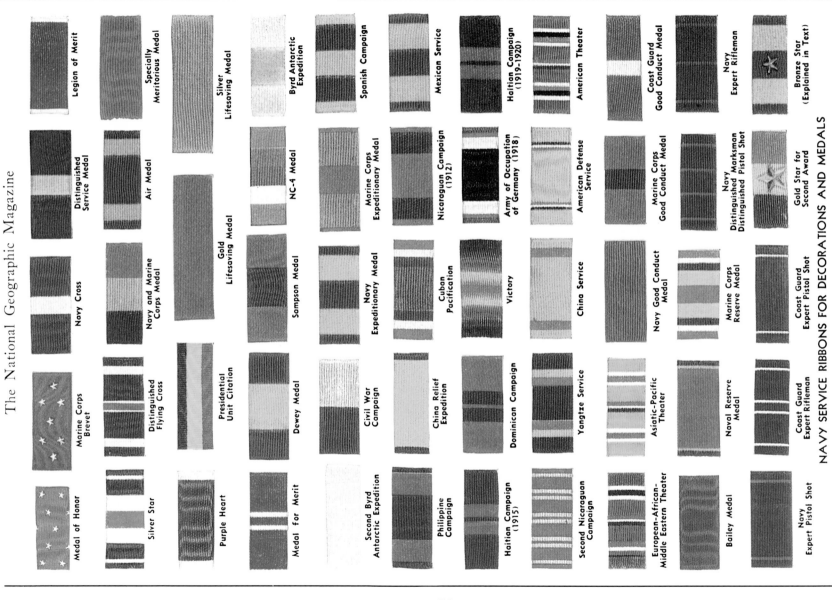

The National Geographic Magazine

NAVY SERVICE RIBBONS FOR DECORATIONS AND MEDALS

Legion of Merit

Specially Meritorious Medal

Silver Lifesaving Medal

Byrd Antarctic Expedition

Spanish Campaign

Mexican Service

Haitian Campaign (1919-1920)

American Theater

Coast Guard Good Conduct Medal

Navy Expert Rifleman

Bronze Star (Explained in Text)

Distinguished Service Medal

Air Medal

NC-4 Medal

Marine Corps Expeditionary Medal

Nicaraguan Campaign (1912)

Army of Occupation of Germany (1918)

American Defense Service

Marine Corps Good Conduct Medal

Navy Distinguished Marksman Distinguished Pistol Shot

Gold Star for Second Award

Navy Cross

Navy and Marine Corps Medal

Gold Lifesaving Medal

Sampson Medal

Navy Expeditionary Medal

Cuban Pacification

Victory

China Service

Navy Good Conduct Medal

Marine Corps Reserve Medal

Marine Corps Brevet

Distinguished Flying Cross

Presidential Unit Citation

Dewey Medal

Civil War Campaign

China Relief Expedition

Dominican Campaign

Yangtze Service

Asiatic-Pacific Theater

Naval Reserve Medal

Coast Guard Expert Pistol Shot

Medal of Honor

Silver Star

Purple Heart

Medal for Merit

Second Byrd Antarctic Expedition

Philippine Campaign

Haitian Campaign (1915)

Second Nicaraguan Campaign

European-African-Middle Eastern Theater

Bailey Medal

Coast Guard Expert Rifleman

Navy Expert Pistol Shot

110

PLATE 95

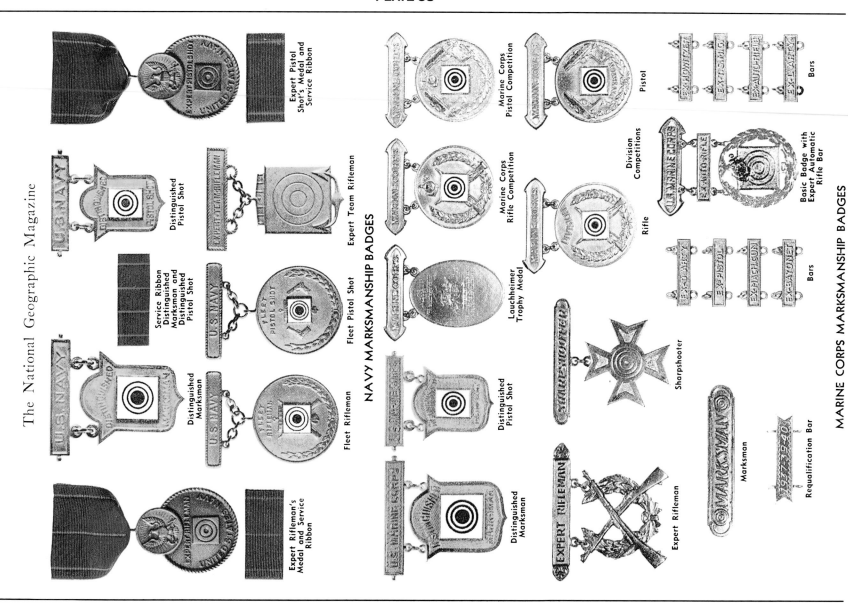

The National Geographic Magazine

**Expert Pistol Shot's Medal and Service Ribbon**

**Distinguished Pistol Shot**

**Expert Team Rifleman**

**Service Ribbon Distinguished Marksman and Distinguished Pistol Shot**

**Fleet Pistol Shot**

**Distinguished Marksman**

**Fleet Rifleman**

**Expert Rifleman's Medal and Service Ribbon**

## NAVY MARKSMANSHIP BADGES

**Marine Corps Pistol Competition**

**Pistol**

**Bars**

**Marine Corps Rifle Competition**

**Division Competitions**

**Basic Badge with Expert Automatic Rifle Bar**

**Lauchheimer Trophy Medal**

**Rifle**

**Bars**

**Distinguished Pistol Shot**

**Sharpshooter**

**Distinguished Marksman**

**Expert Rifleman**

**Marksman**

**Requalification Bar**

## MARINE CORPS MARKSMANSHIP BADGES

**PLATE 96**

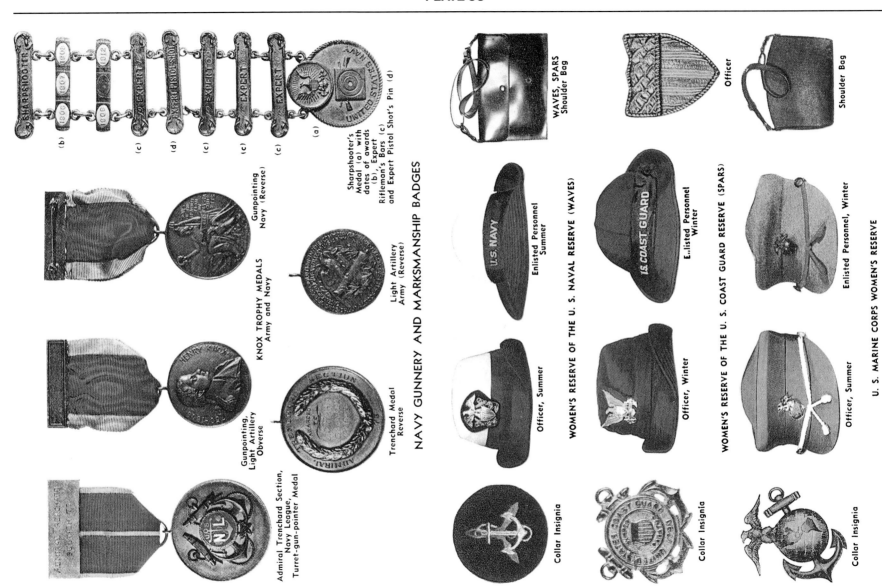

## NAVY GUNNERY AND MARKSMANSHIP BADGES

Sharpshooter's Medal (a) with dates of awards (b), Expert Rifleman's Bars (c) and Expert Pistol Shot's Pin (d)

KNOX TROPHY MEDALS
Army and Navy

Gunpointing, Navy (Reverse)

Light Artillery Army (Reverse)

Gunpointing, Light Artillery Obverse

Trenchard Medal Reverse

Admiral Trenchard Section, Navy League, Turret-gun-pointer Medal

WAVES, SPARS Shoulder Bag

Officer

Shoulder Bag

Enlisted Personnel Summer

Officer, Summer

**WOMEN'S RESERVE OF THE U. S. NAVAL RESERVE (WAVES)**

Collar Insignia

Enlisted Personnel Winter

Officer, Winter

**WOMEN'S RESERVE OF THE U. S. COAST GUARD RESERVE (SPARS)**

Collar Insignia

Enlisted Personnel, Winter

Officer, Summer

**U. S. MARINE CORPS WOMEN'S RESERVE**

Collar Insignia